HUMANITY IN THE STREETS

NEW YORK CITY 1960s–1980s

BUILDER LEVY

HUMANITY IN THE STREETS

NEW YORK CITY 1960s–1980s

Builder Levy
Humanity in the Streets: New York City 1960s–1980s

Editing: Alice Deutsch

Published by Damiani
info@damianieditore.com
www.damianieditore.com

Printed in 2018 by Grafiche Damiani – Faenza Group SpA, Italy.

ISBN 978-88-6208-612-7

FOREWORD

Builder Levy's *Humanity in the Streets* speaks of New York City and photography in a classic way. His topics range from community building, girls play, fashion, protest movements, boys playing, rooftops, pigeons to the beauty shop. Levy crosses boundaries set by the landscape of the city and by social unrests. His visual stories are easy to reimagine and at the same time complex in their framing. The black and white photographs speak of multiple identities found in the city as he questions and affirms the notion of humanity by showing men and women arm in arm offering a unified stance on issues. We see black and white, men and women, girls and boys; we note the racial and economic diversity of a neighborhood through the signage as residents demand change. The faces of Latinos and Latinas are brilliantly framed through his lens along with celebrities and political leaders. Levy is a close reader of people and a keen observer to events. He is quick and he is steady as he shapes a story about protest and the everyday. He questions what it means to be non-violent when arms surround a young black man's neck in a menacing way. In a crowd scene, we see police in uniform as a group fills the frame at a train station in Flushing, young students in Brooklyn hold signs demanding an education that is fair and just; families in Coney Island share moments of joy and pleasure while Veterans of war mobilize for a peaceful resolution in Vietnam. Playgrounds, parks, handball and basketball courts fill the pages as empty lots show the devastation of a once vibrant community. Dr. Martin Luther King, Jr. is here with members of the Black Panther Party as young boys read political journals like *Freedomways* while others read the Black Panther Party news; housewives and grandmothers; fathers and workers; teenagers play cards as a group of sharply dressed young men wearing hats and sunglasses pose for the photographer. In 1965, they were called the Medallion Lords; one imagines how visible they were as they filled the sidewalk with their stylish coats and hats. There is a sense of collaboration with the people who are not invisible to the photographer. It is a remarkable visual story about beauty and humanity that must not be overlooked.

Deborah Willis

PREFACE

I grew up in Brooklyn during the Cold War and the McCarthy era in a family that encouraged art and believed we needed a world without war and hate, racism, sexism, exploitation and poverty. To this day, those beliefs have remained with me.

As an art major at Brooklyn College, I thought of myself as an abstract expressionist. At the same time, I felt a need for a direct connection to the social realities of life in the city, nation, and world. I wanted to be immersed in the life and struggles of the day. The paintings I made at Brooklyn College and the welded steel 'junk' sculpture I made in graduate school, did not fulfill my need for a strong social connection in my art. But with photography it was different. It took me out into the streets, where, with the mediation of the camera, I could and did immerse myself directly into real life. I attended rallies and marches for civil rights, peace and justice. With camera in hand, I tried to visually capture the emotional and ideological experiences in which I too, was a partisan participant. I wandered through the Lower East Side before gentrification. I returned to Coney Island—always teeming with multitudes—which I remembered from my childhood visits. After college, my camera was ready when I moved out to multiracial, multiclass Clinton Hill. I brought it with me to work when I got a job as a recreation leader at P.S. 20 playground in nearby Fort Greene. I explored the streets of Bedford-Stuyvesant, photographing for the Pratt Institute Planning Department which worked with local organizations to save and rehabilitate old buildings. As a New York City teacher, I set up photography workshop programs, first in Ocean Hill Brownsville, and several years later, in an alternative high school program in Bushwick (for thirteen years), and after that in another alternative high school program in the Jacob Riis Housing Project on the Lower East Side. As part of each of these workshop programs, the students, armed with workshop cameras, explored and photographed in their neighborhoods, on their blocks, and in their homes. And I went with them and photographed too.

With the camera, I could abstract, compose, and intensify aspects of often chaotic, fluid reality within the rectangle of my viewfinder. With the release of the shutter, I could begin to physically create a new consciousness in and of the world. Photography made it possible for me to become the artist that I wanted to be—seeking possibilities of a better world within the quotidian life and enduring humanity in the streets of New York City.

Builder Levy

HUMANITY IN THE STREETS

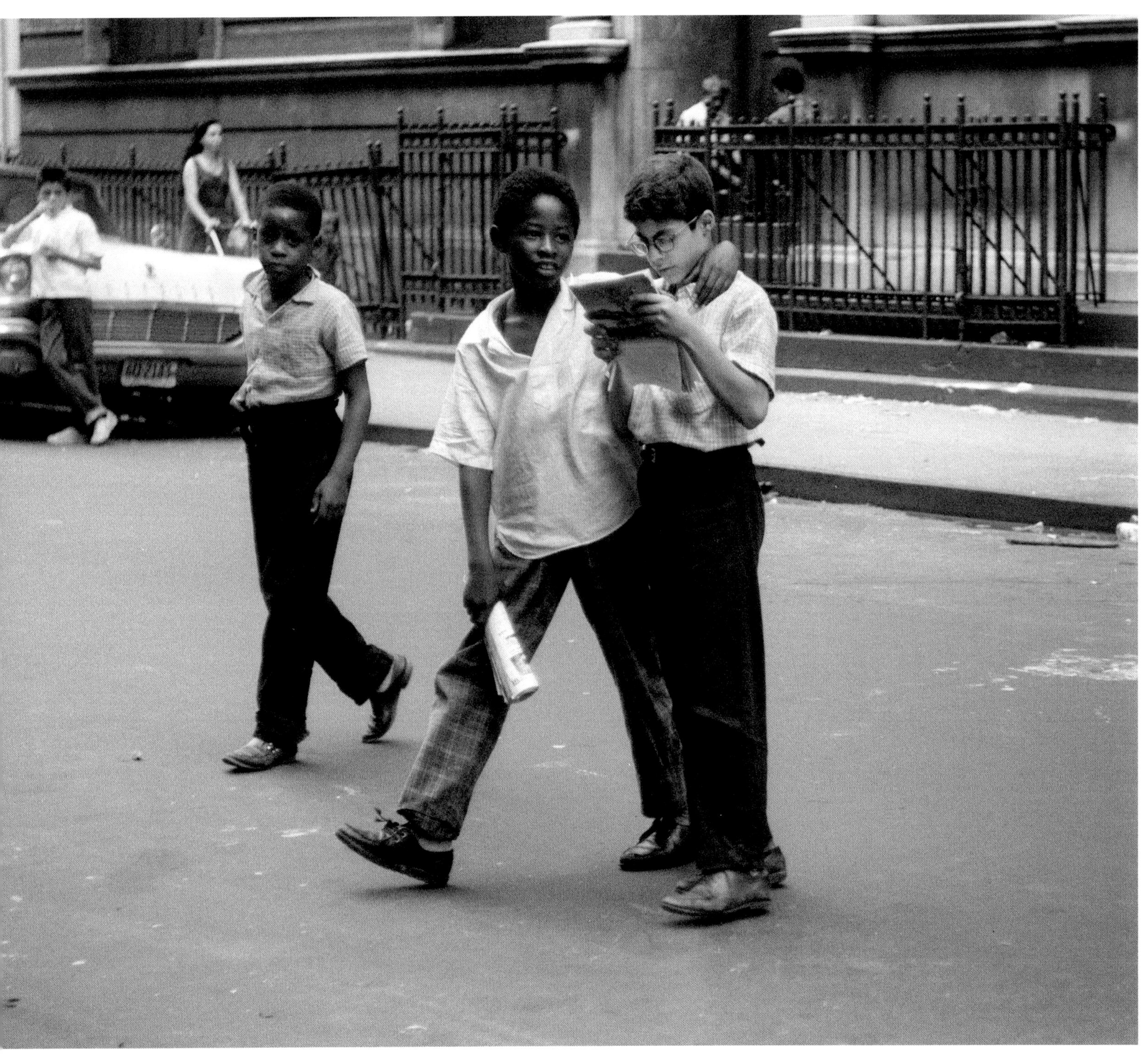

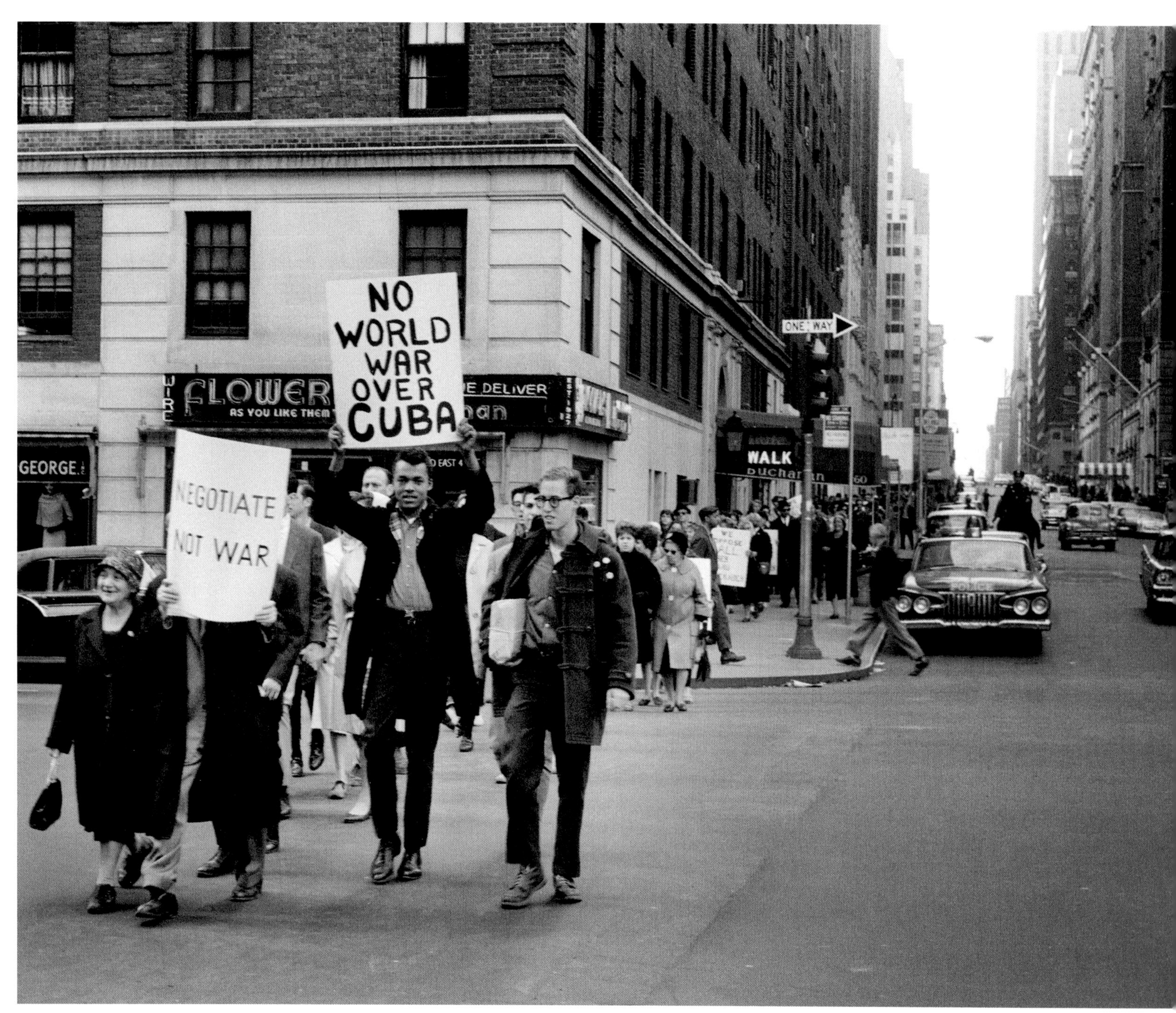

NO WORLD WAR OVER CUBA
NEGOTIATE NOT WAR
FLOWER
AS YOU LIKE THEM
WIRE
WE DELIVER
GEORGE
WALK
ONE WAY
POLICE

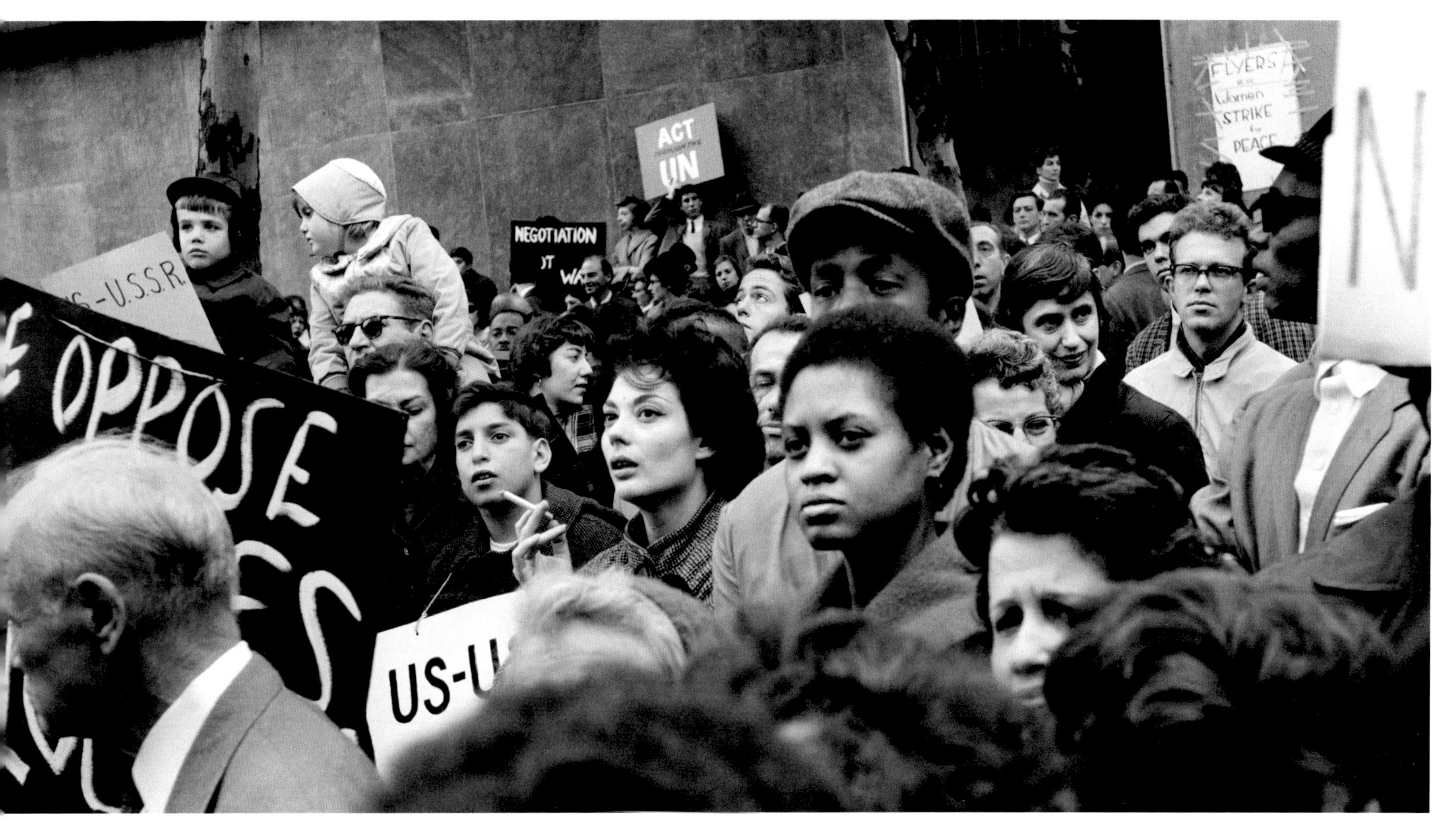
US-U.S.S.R.
OPPOSE
US-U
NEGOTIATION
T WA
ACT
UN
FLYERS
Women
STRIKE
PEACE
N

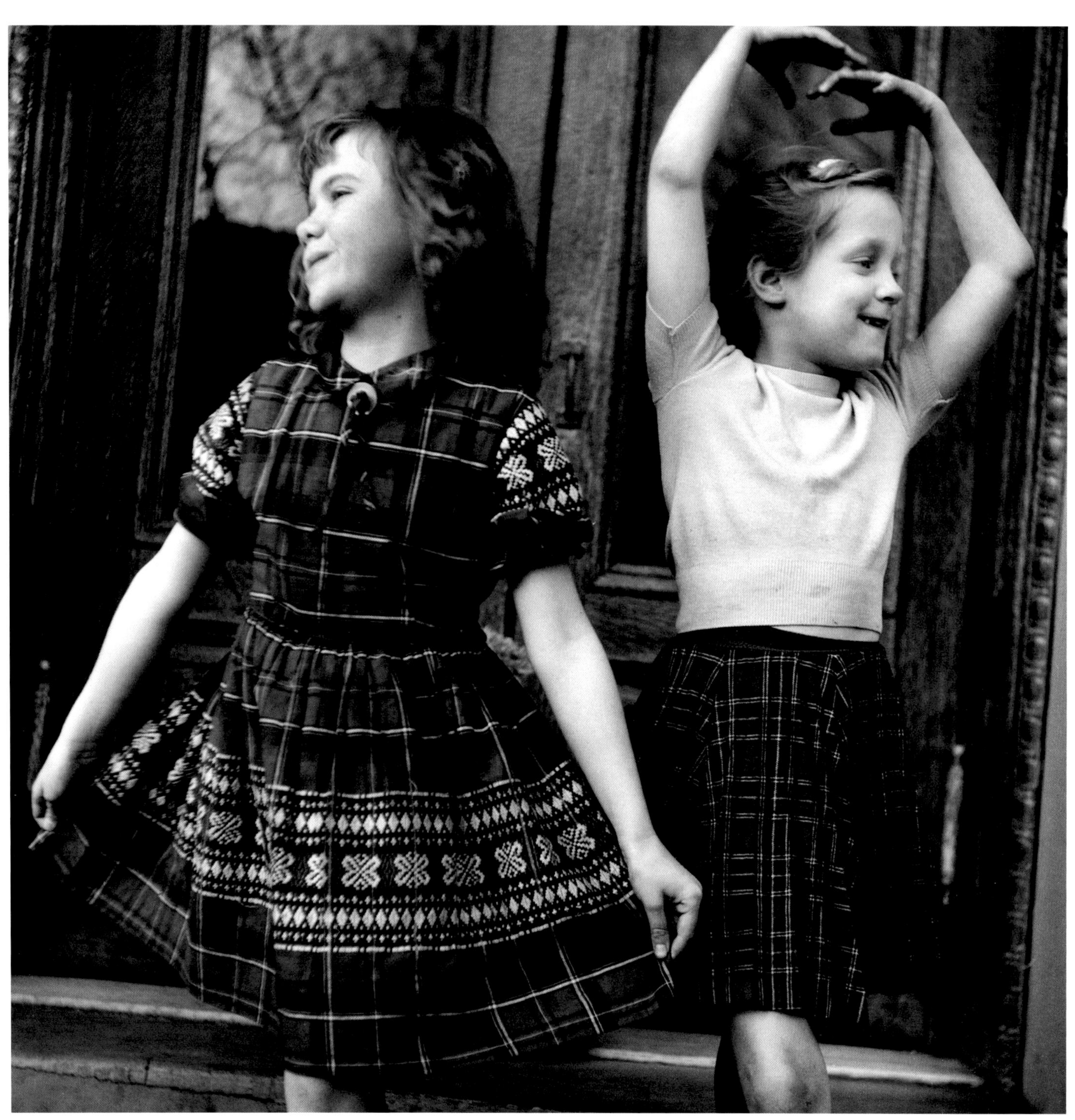

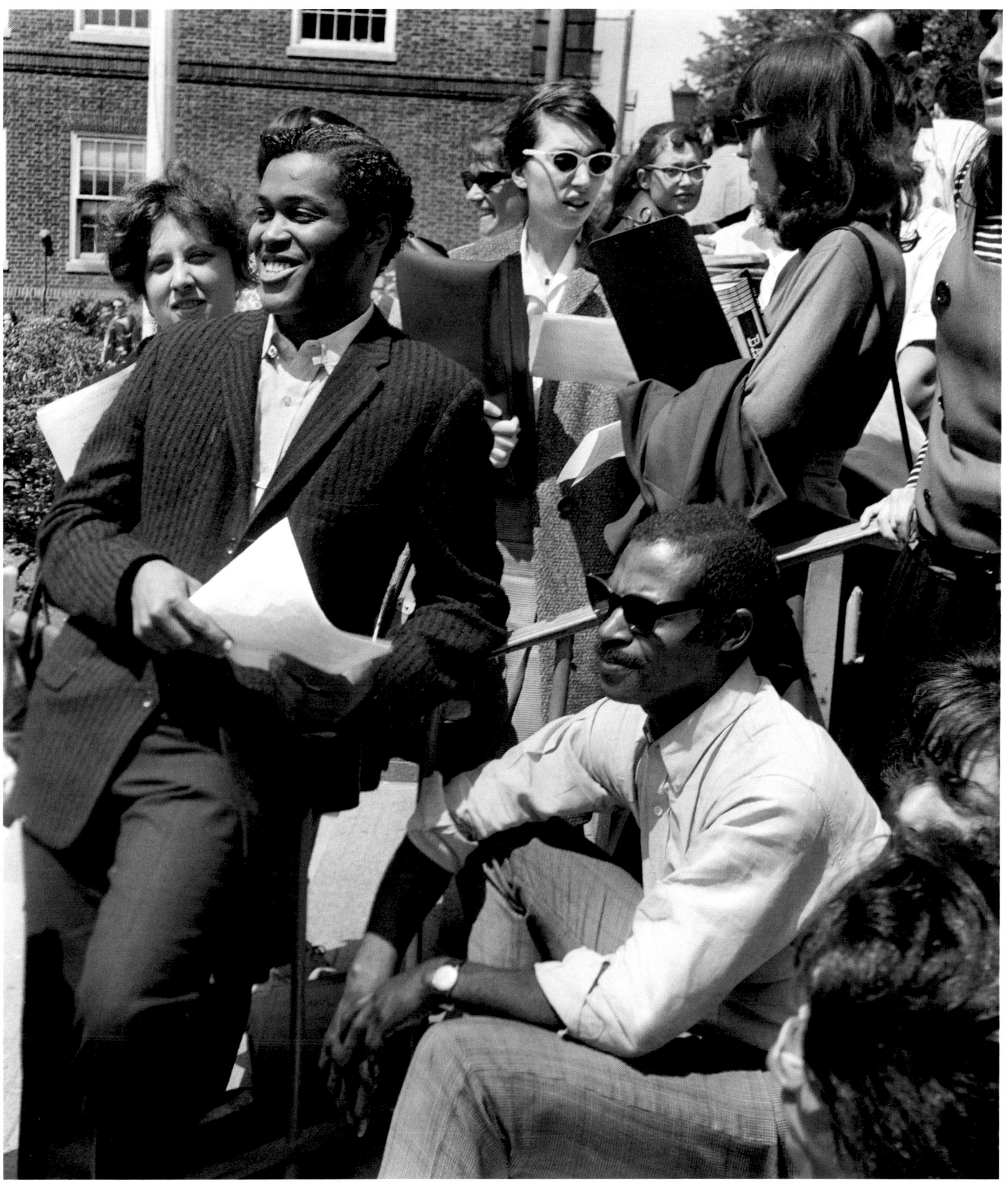

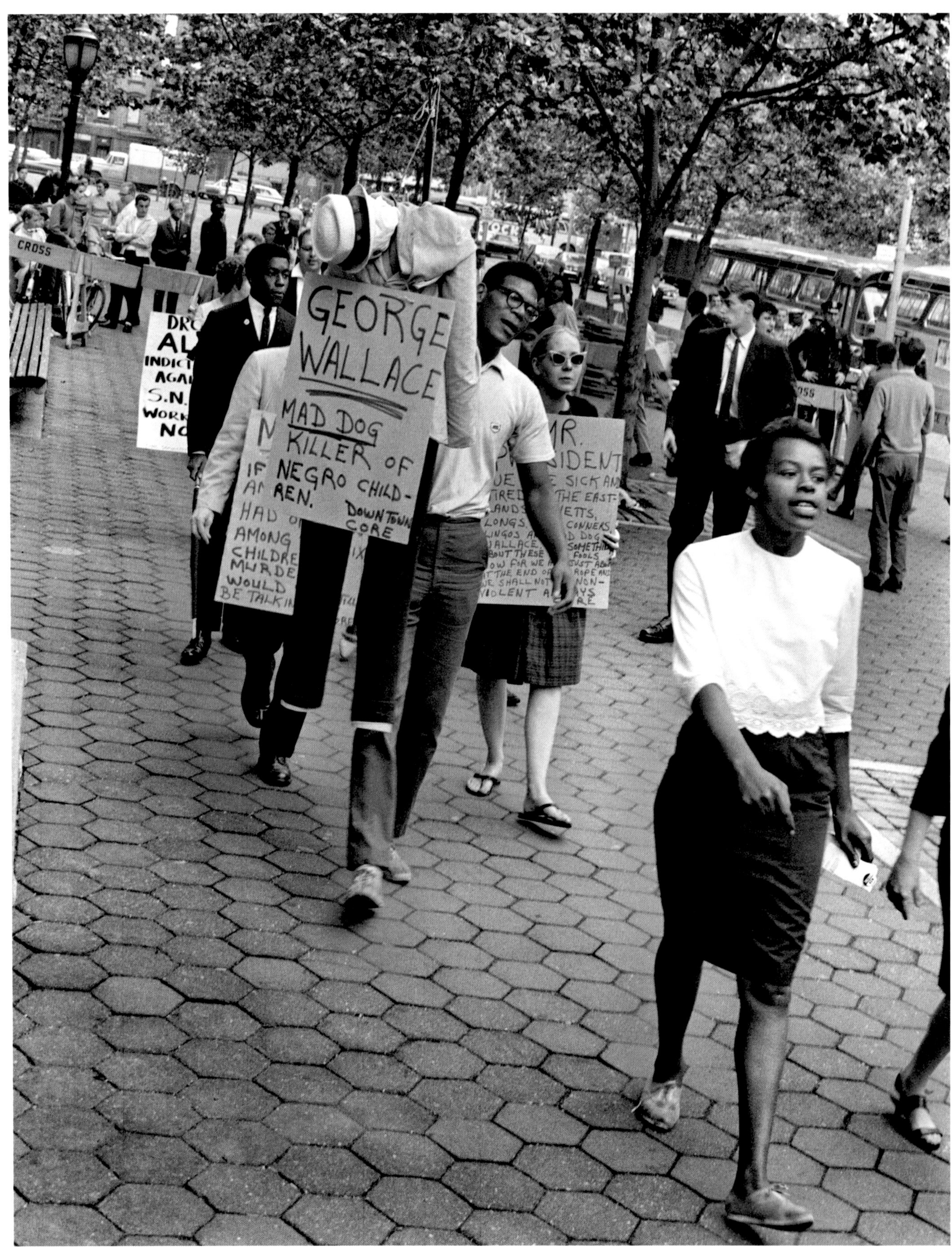
CROSS
DRO
AL
INDICT
AGAI
S.N.
WORN
NO
GEORGE
WALLACE
MAD DOG
KILLER OF
NEGRO CHILD-
REN.
IF
AM
HAD
AMONG
CHILDRE
MURDE
WOULD
BE TALKIN
DOWN TOWN
CORE
MR.
PRESIDENT
SICK AN
TIRED THE EAST
LANDS ETTS.
LONGS   CONNERS
LINGOS A D DOG
WALLACE, SOMETHI
OUT THESE FOOLS
OW FAR WE JUST A
THE END O ROPE AND
WE SHALL NOT NON-
VIOLENT A AYS
RE

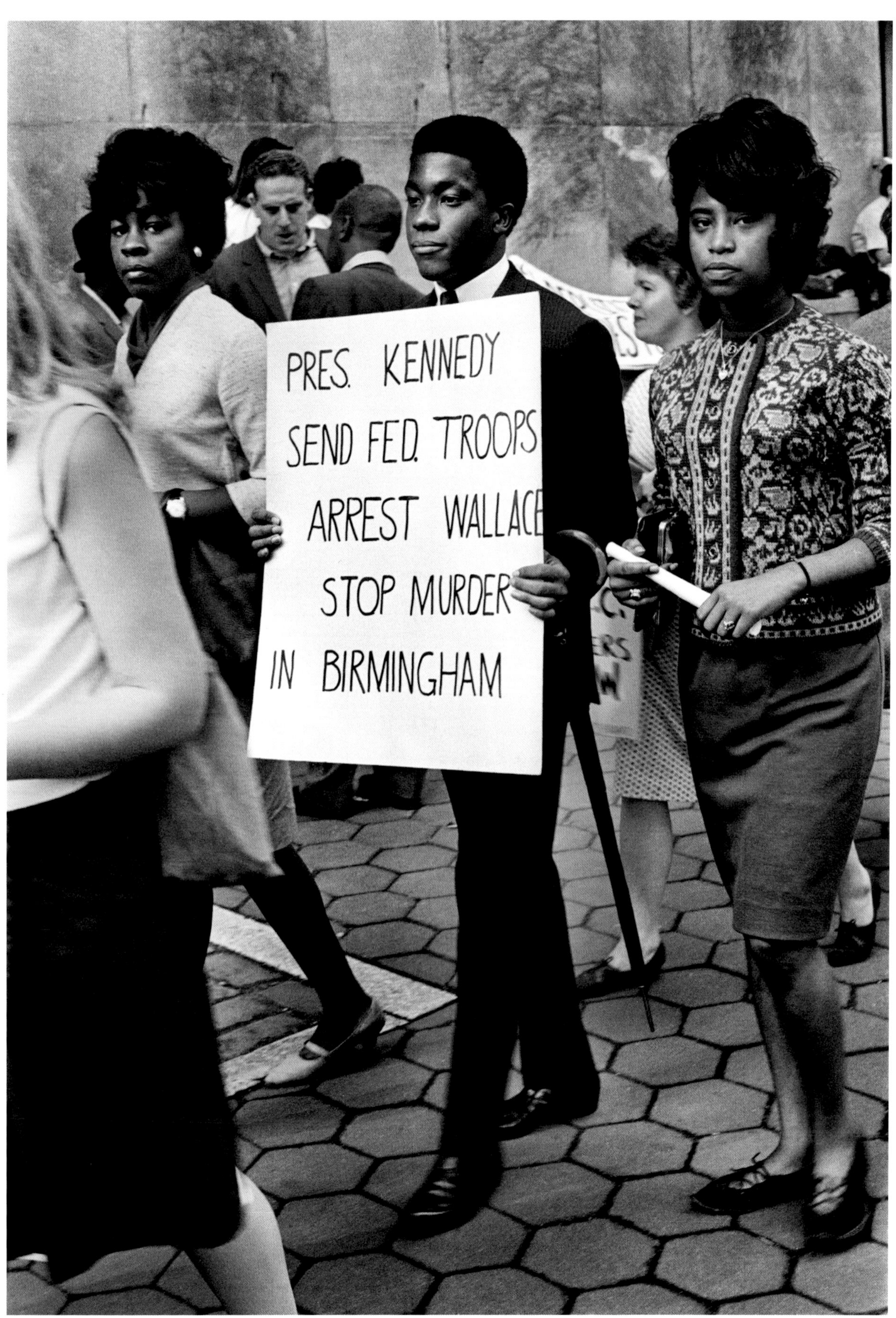

PRES. KENNEDY
SEND FED. TROOPS
ARREST WALLACE
STOP MURDER
IN BIRMINGHAM

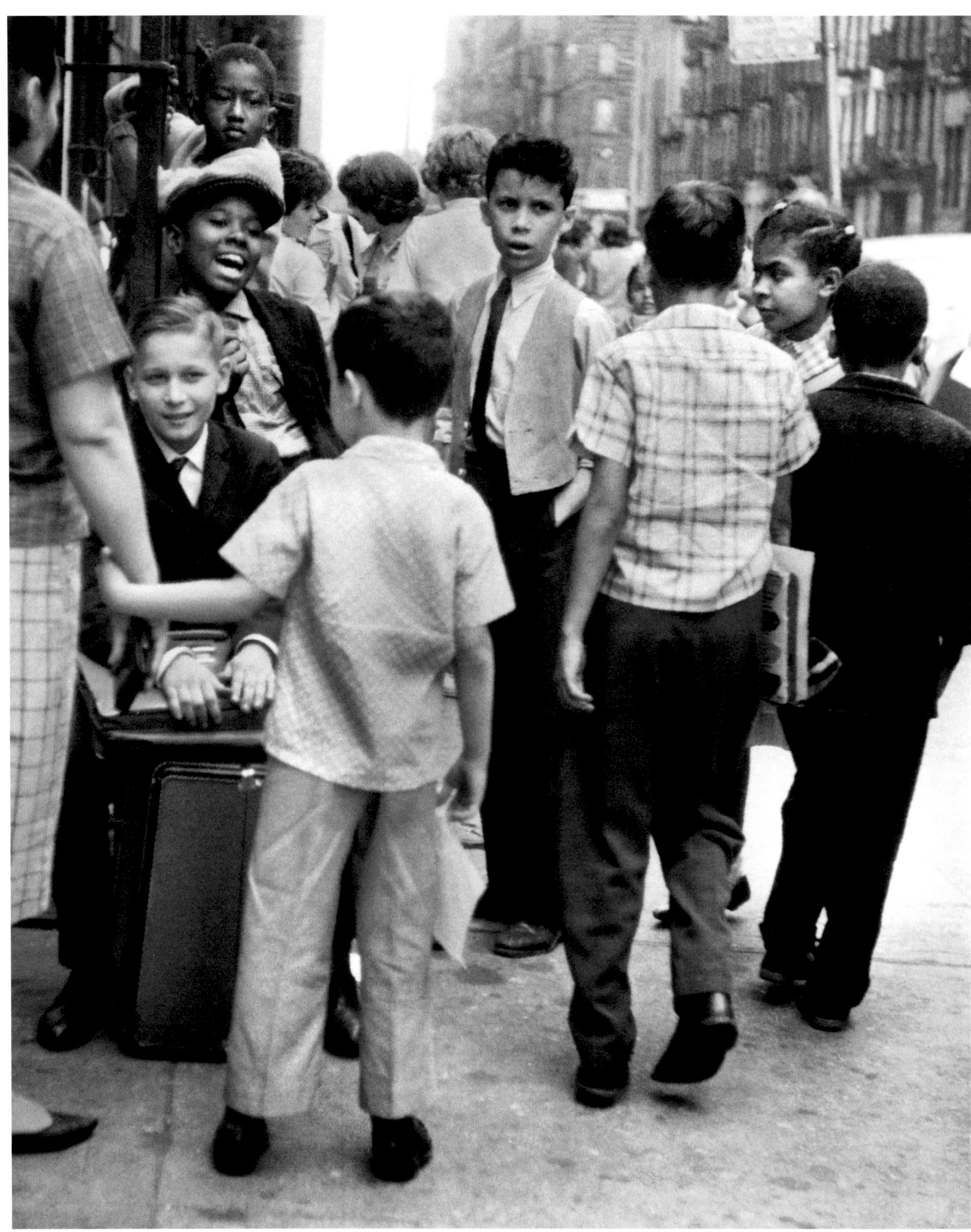

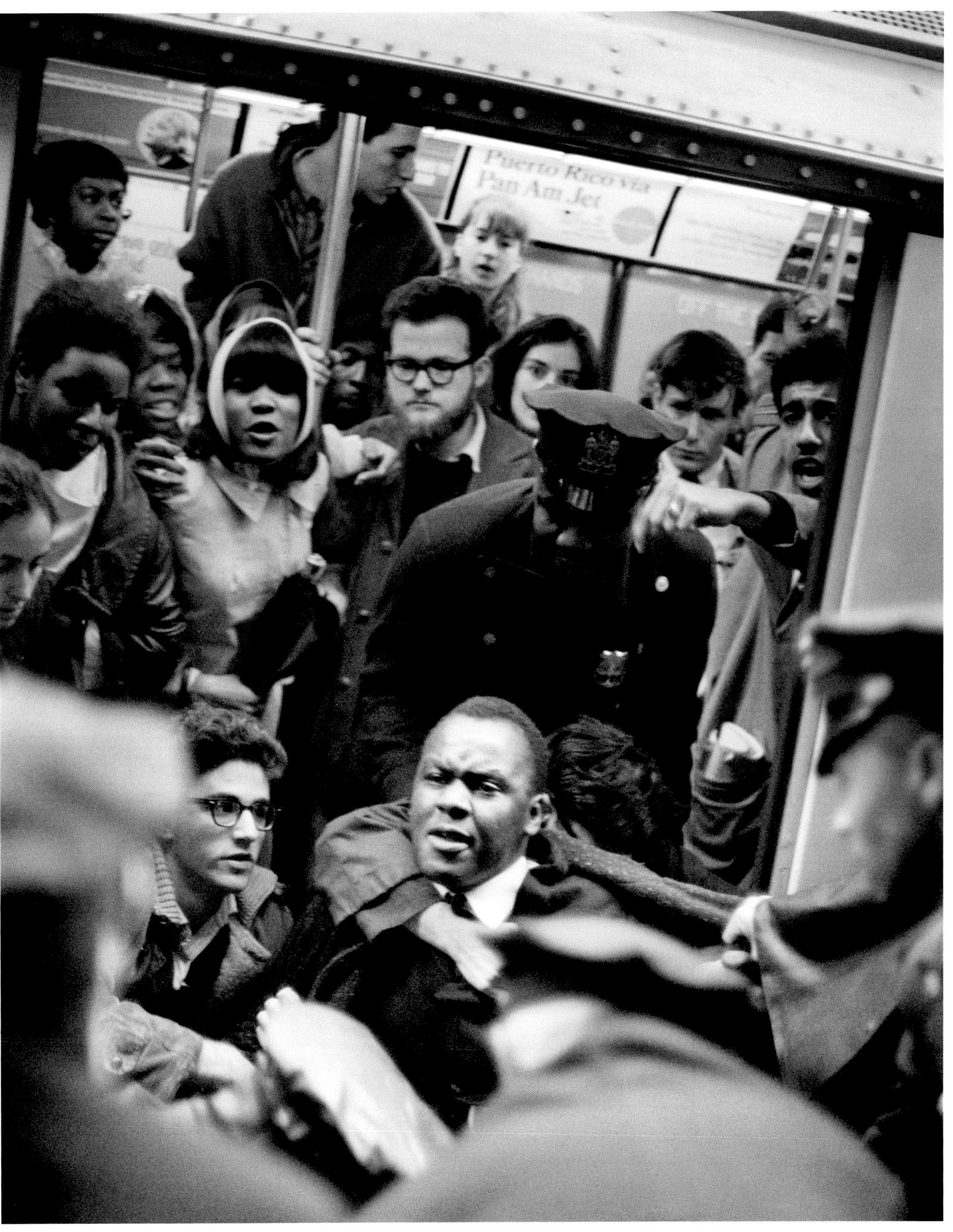
Puerto Rico via
Pan Am Jet

CITYWIDE SCHOOL BOYCOTT

In 1954 the Supreme Court of the United States declared segregated schools unconstitutional. Ten years later, a coalition of New York City civil rights, community, and labor union groups organized a citywide school boycott on February 3, 1964. Over 460,000 students stayed out of school, protesting inadequate, separate and unequal education, and demanding integrated schools, high quality education, and an end to (de facto) school segregation in New York City.

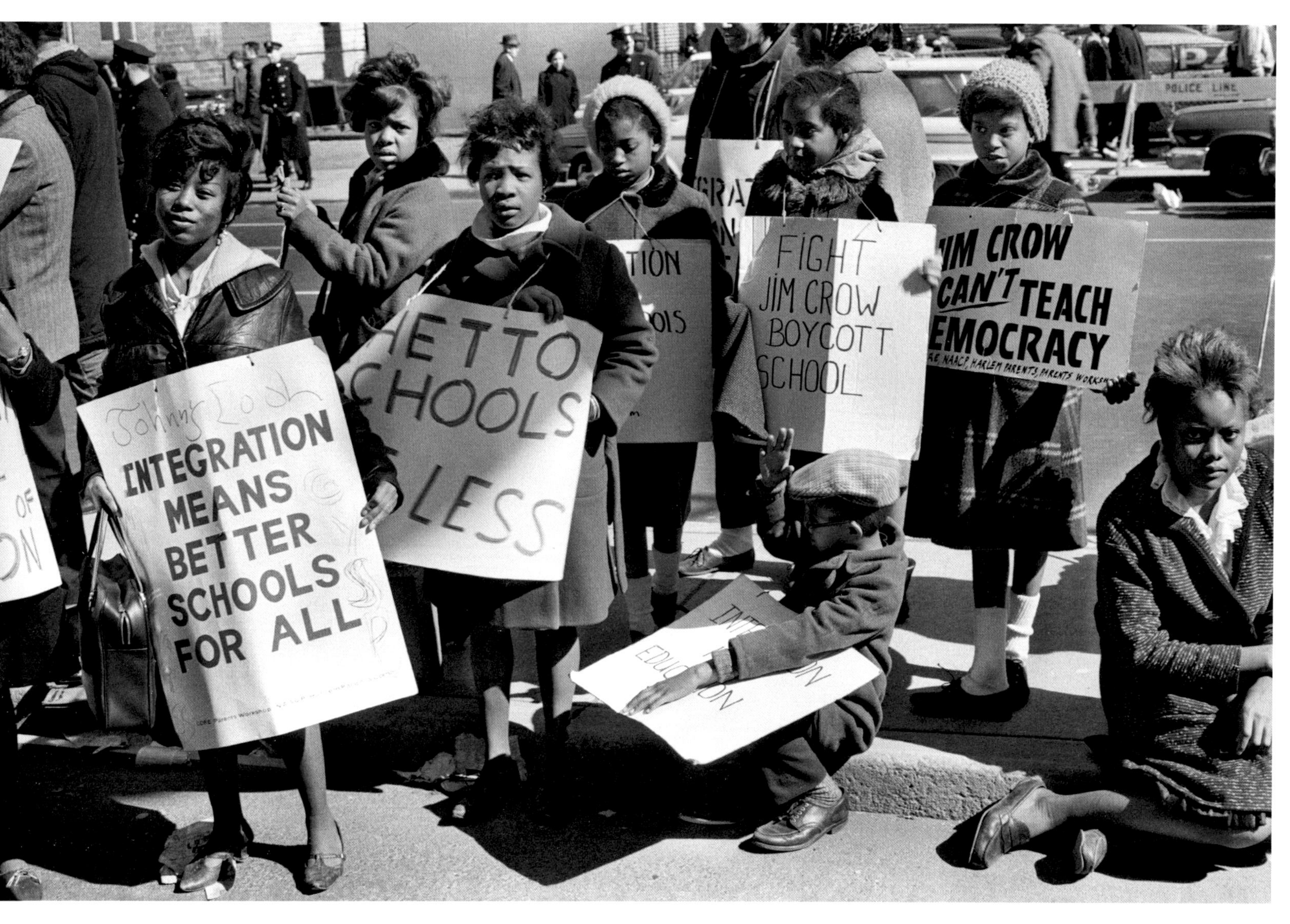
Johnny Cool
INTEGRATION
MEANS
BETTER
SCHOOLS
FOR ALL
GHETTO
SCHOOLS
LESS
FIGHT
JIM CROW
BOYCOTT
SCHOOL
JIM CROW
CAN'T TEACH
DEMOCRACY
NAACP HARLEM PARENTS PARENTS WORKERS
EDUCATION

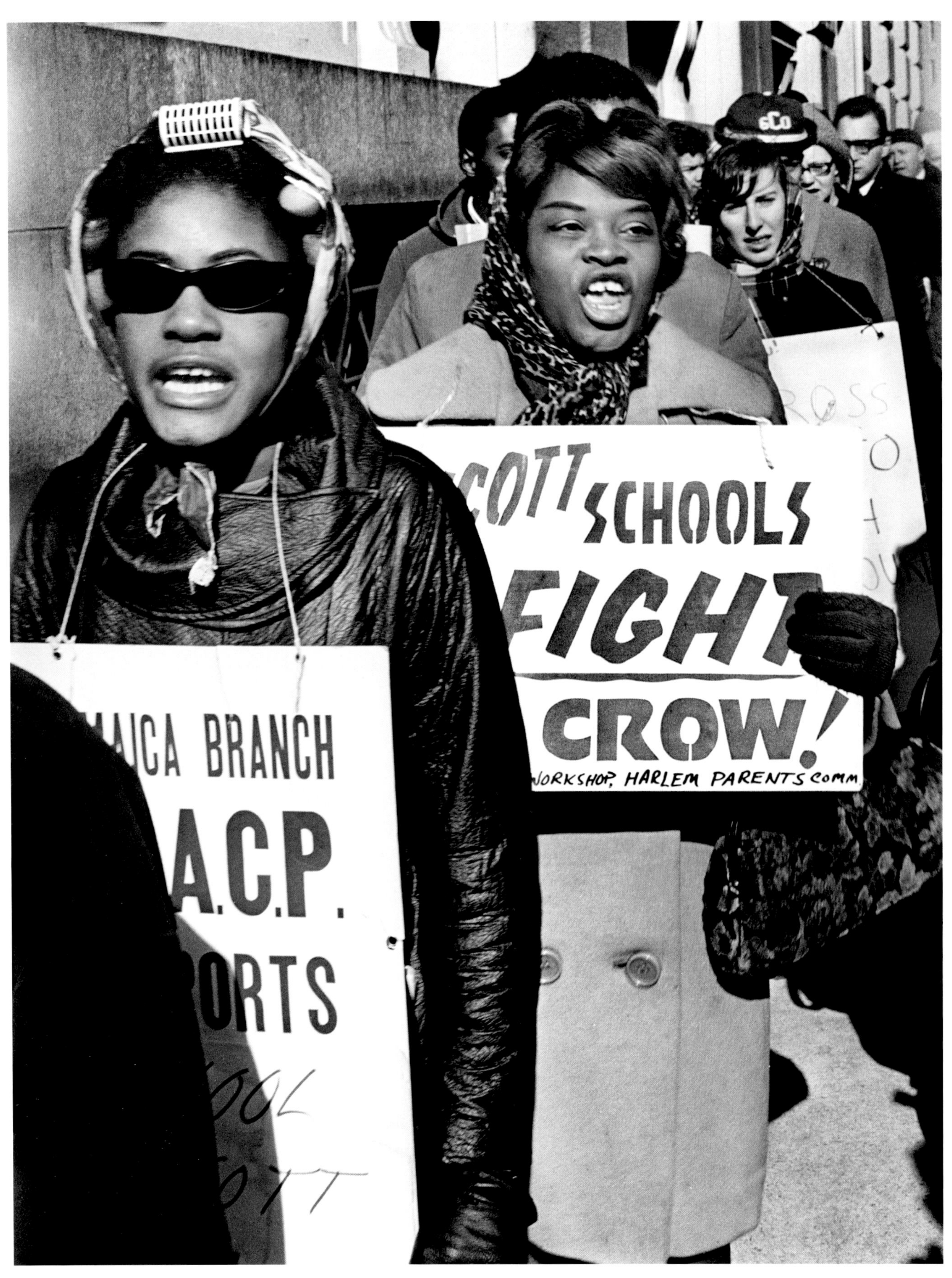
SCOTT SCHOOLS
FIGHT
CROW!
WORKSHOP, HARLEM PARENTS COMM.
JAMAICA BRANCH
N.A.C.P.
PORTS

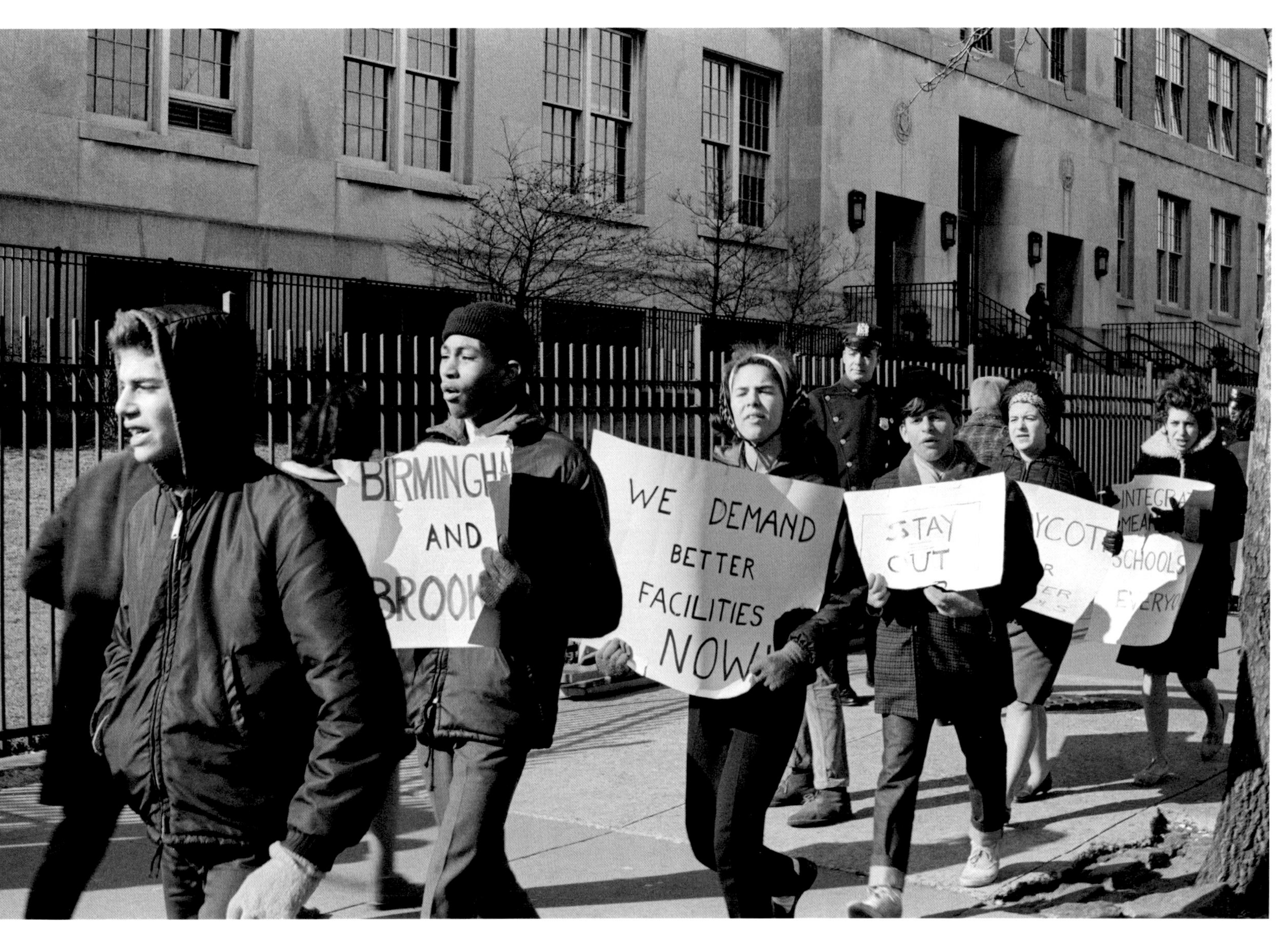
BIRMINGHAM
AND
BROOK
WE DEMAND
BETTER
FACILITIES
NOW
STAY
OUT
YCOTT
INTEGRA
MEA
SCHOOLS
EVERY

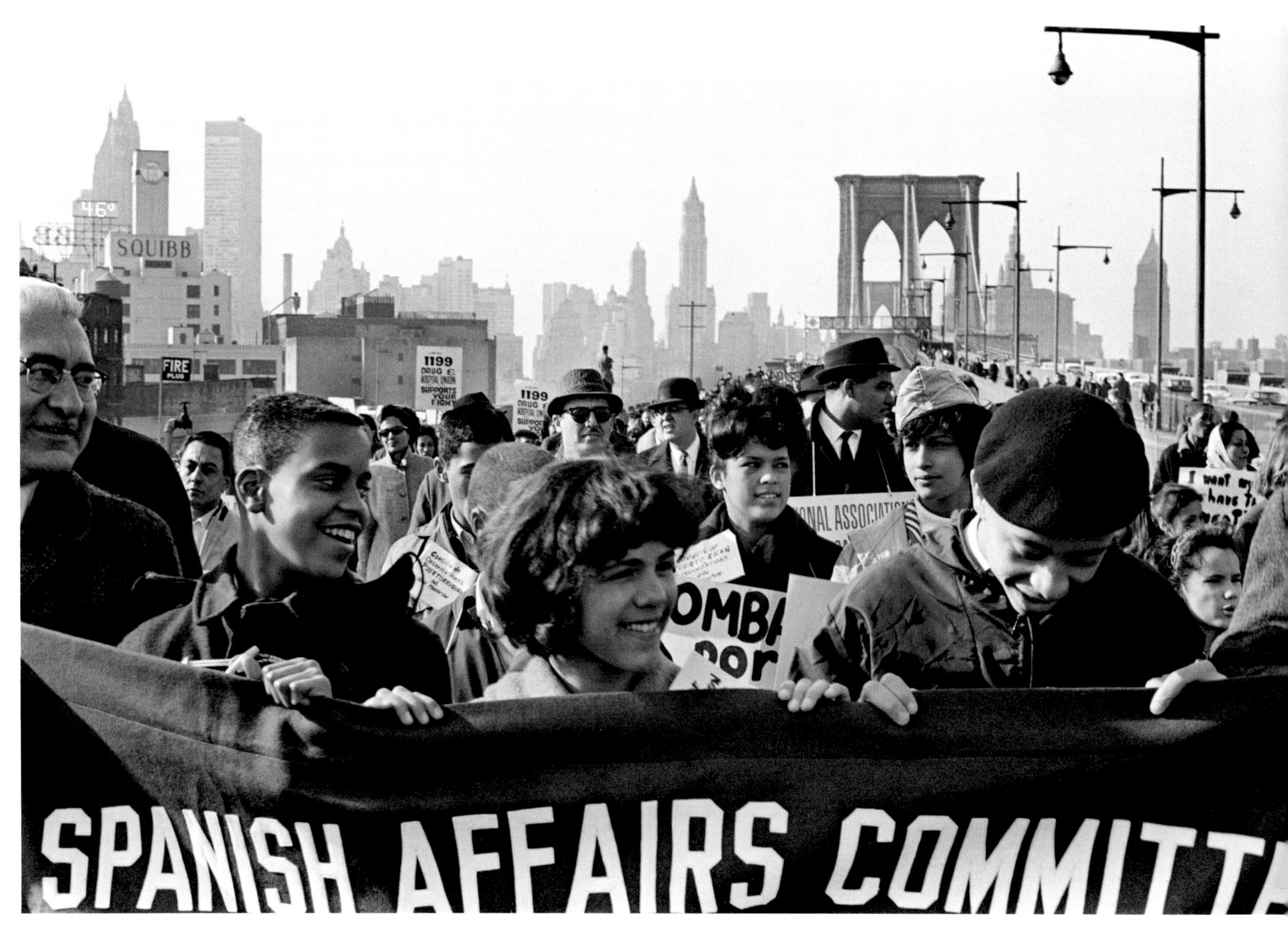
SQUIBB
46°
FIRE PLUS
1199 DRUG & HOSPITAL UNION SUPPORTS YOUR FIGHT
SPANISH AFFAIRS COMMITT

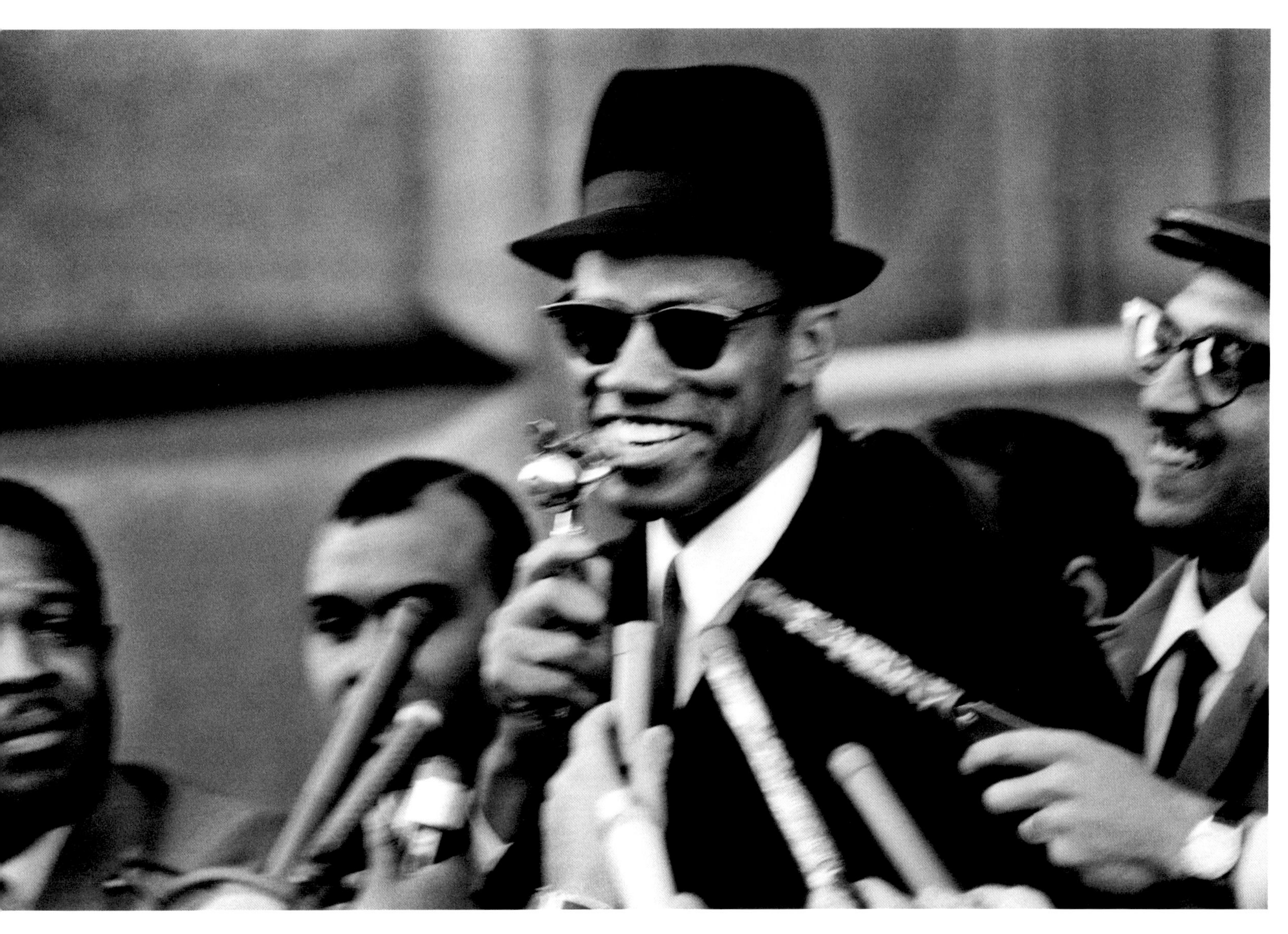

CONEY ISLAND

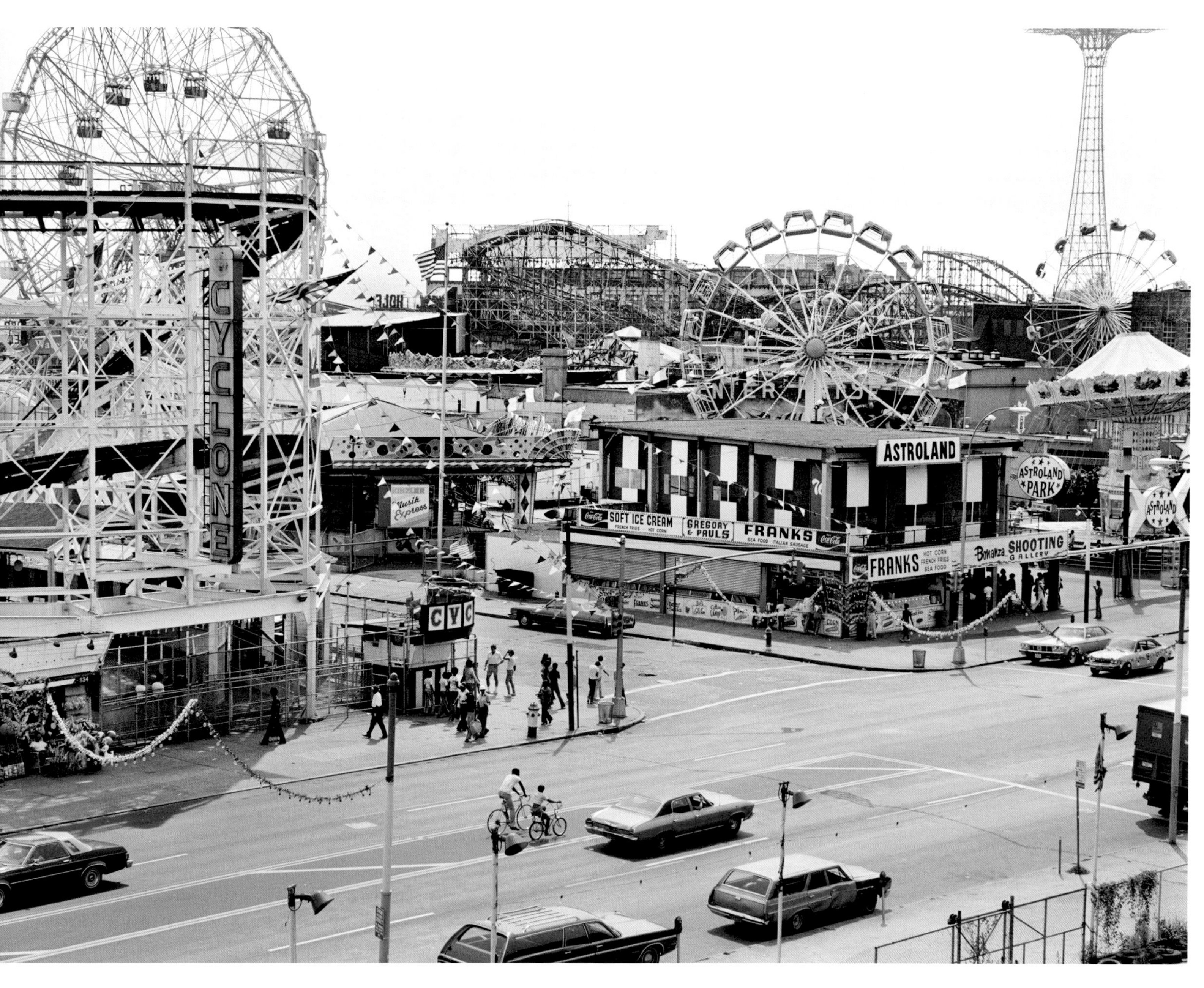

CYCLONE
ASTROLAND
ASTROLAND PARK
ASTROLAND
SOFT ICE CREAM
FRENCH FRIES · HOT CORN
GREGORY & PAULS
FRANKS
SEA FOOD · ITALIAN SAUSAGE
Coca-Cola
FRANKS
HOT CORN
FRENCH FRIES
SEA FOOD
Bonanza SHOOTING GALLERY
CYC

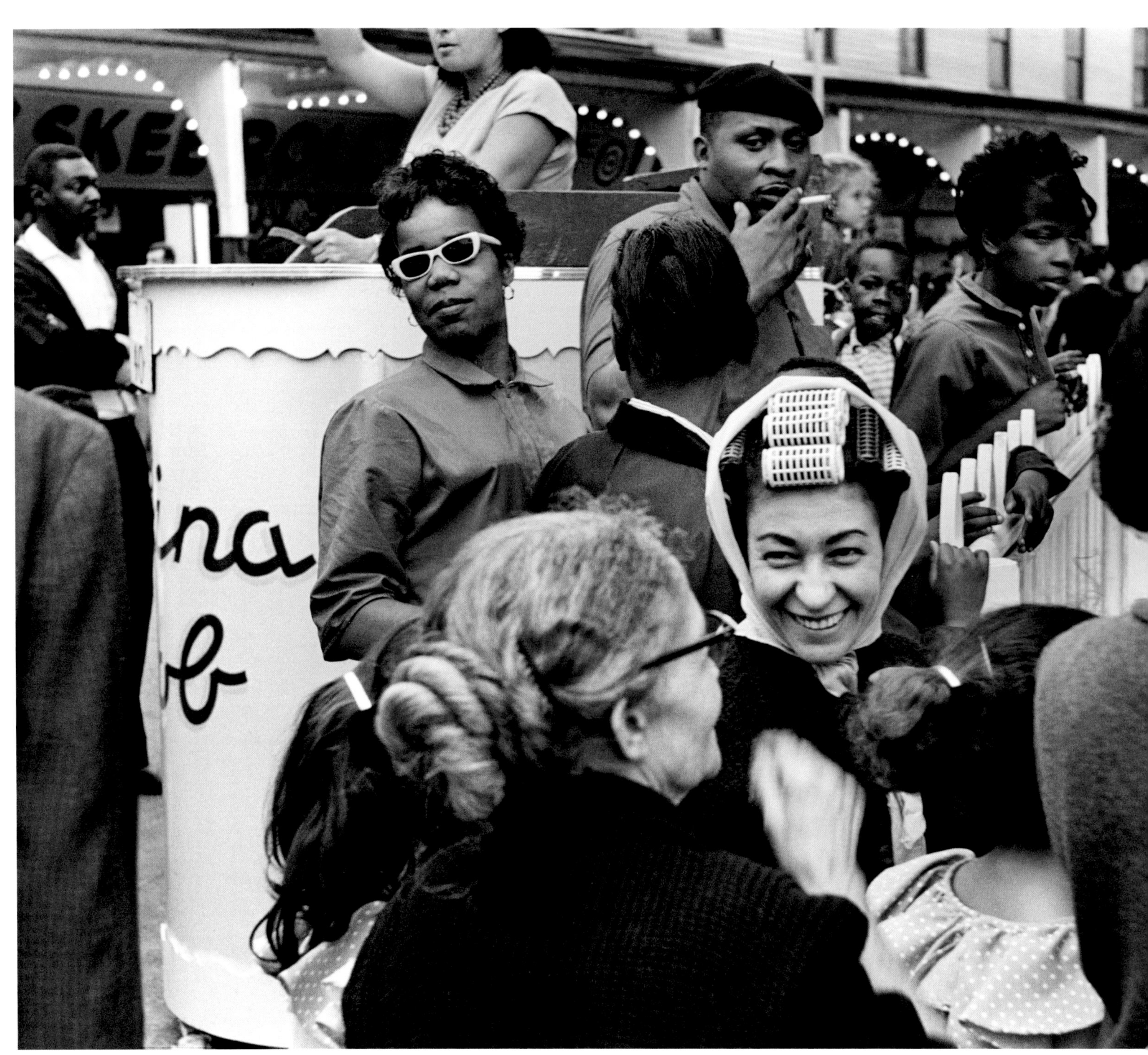
SKEE
ina
b

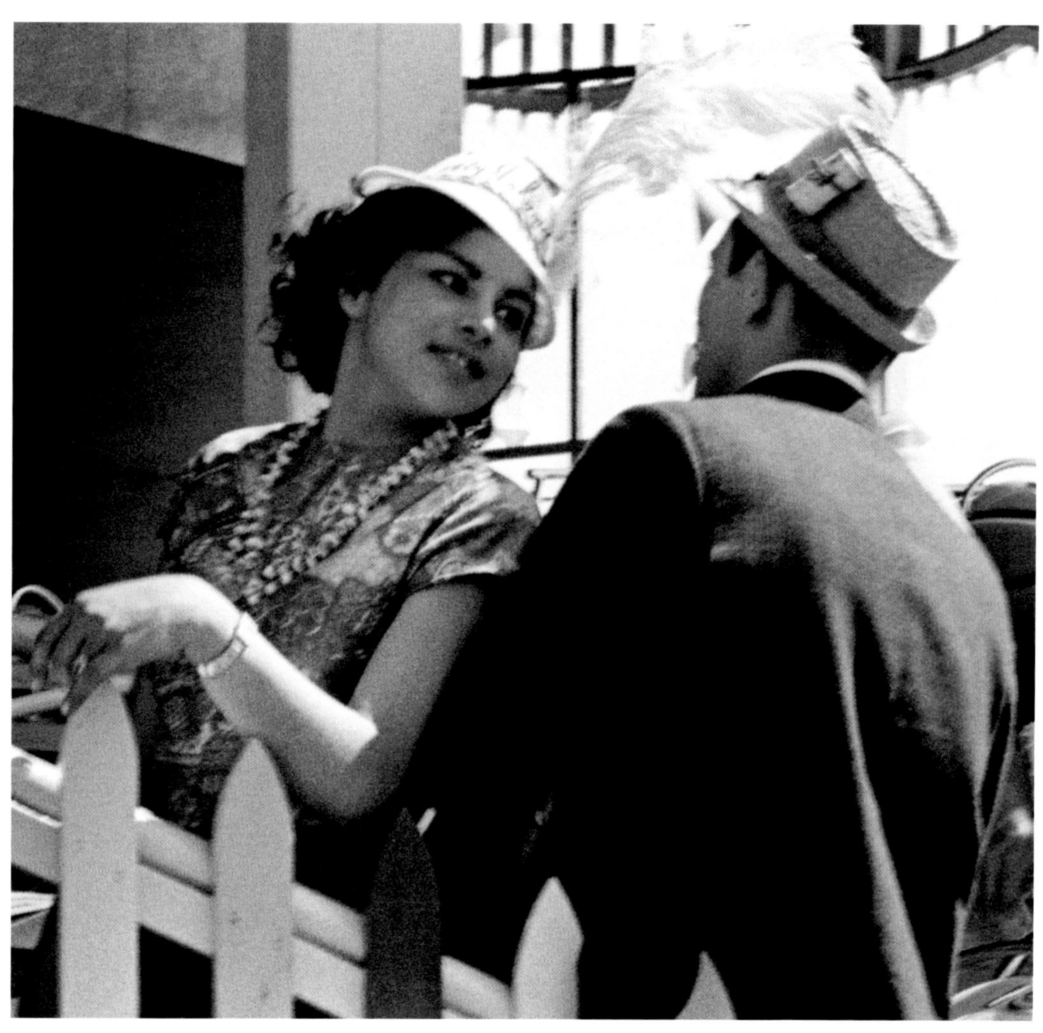

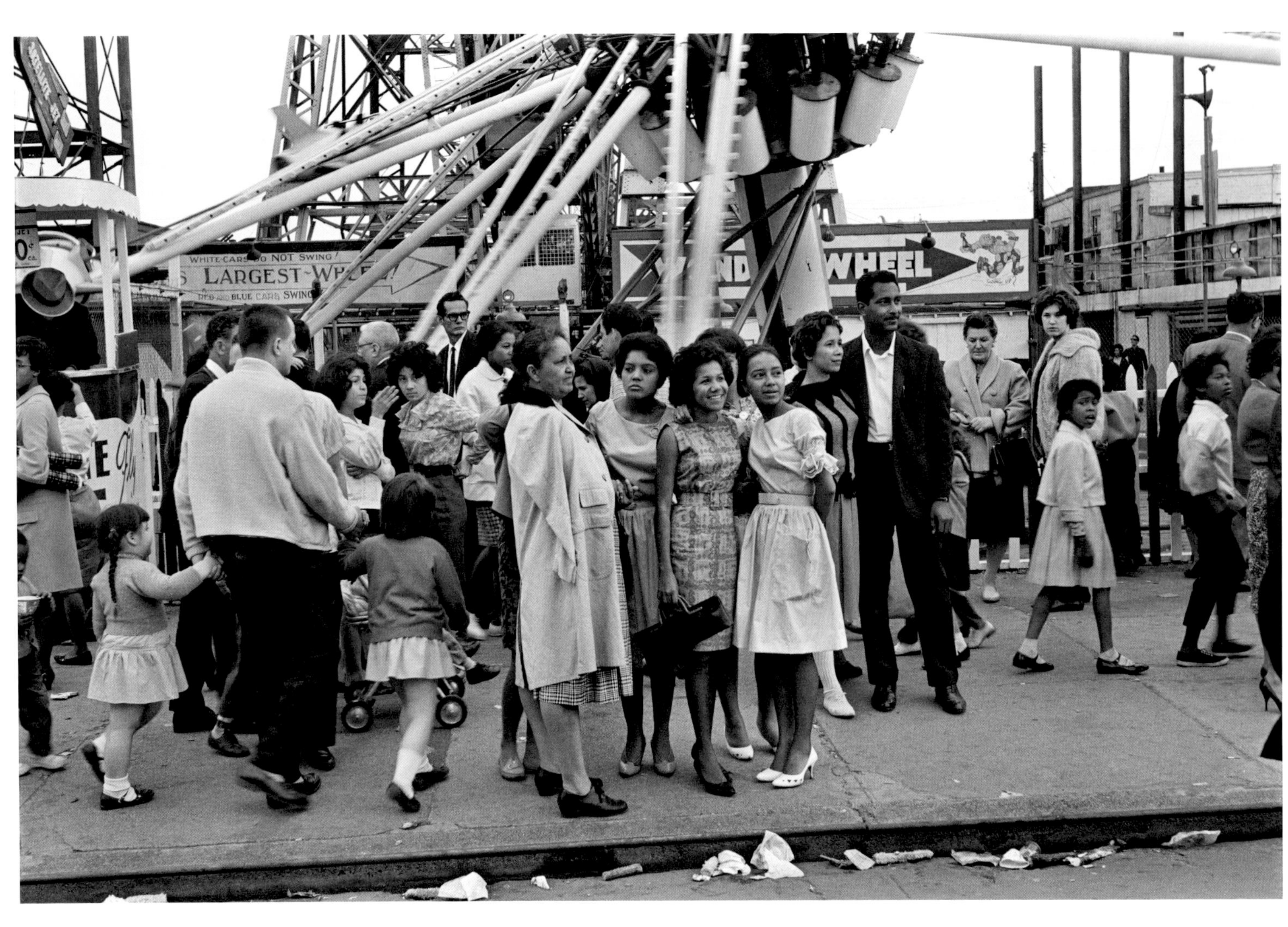
WHITE CARS DO NOT SWING
LARGEST WHEEL
RED AND BLUE CARS SWING
WONDER WHEEL

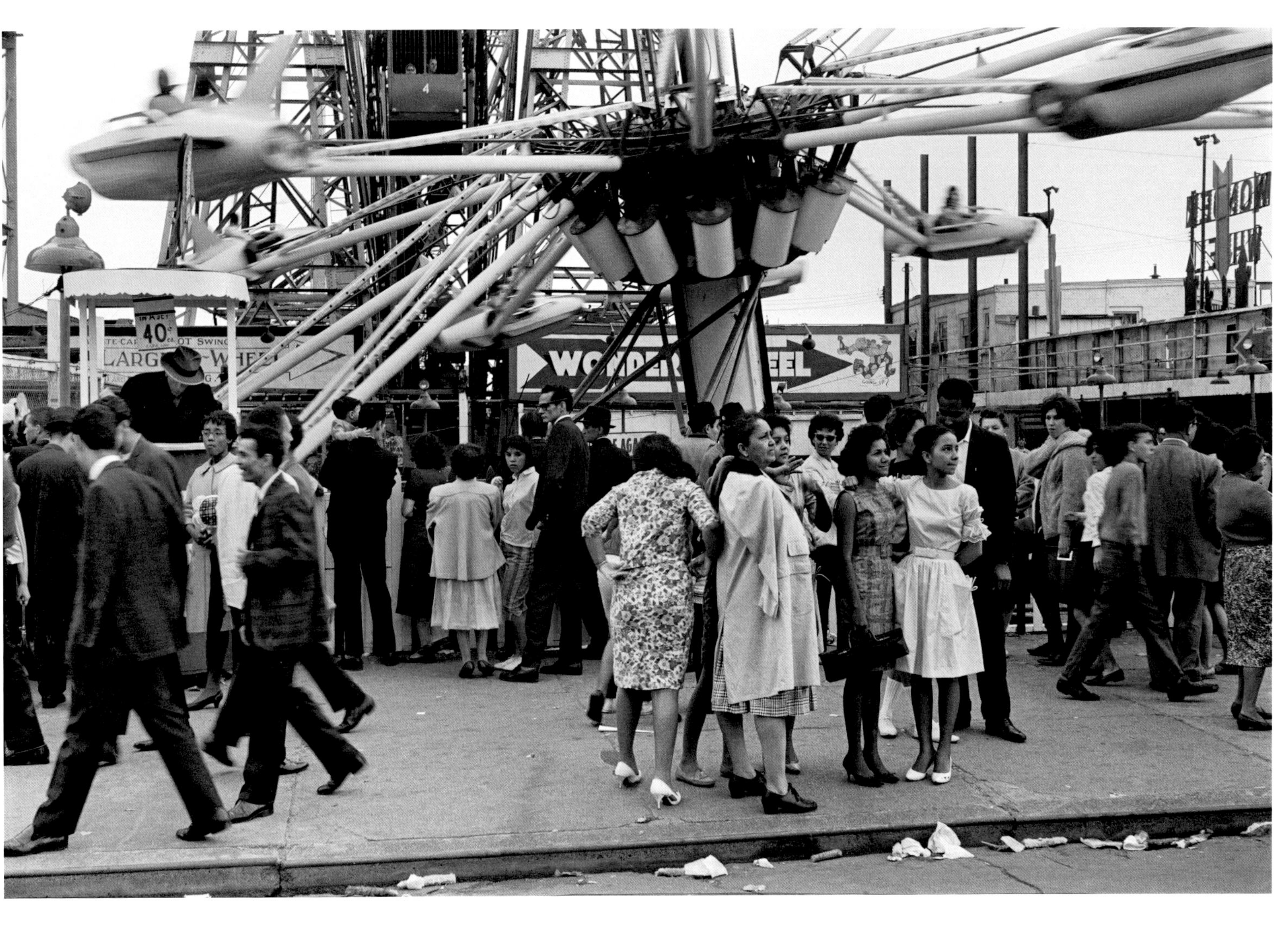

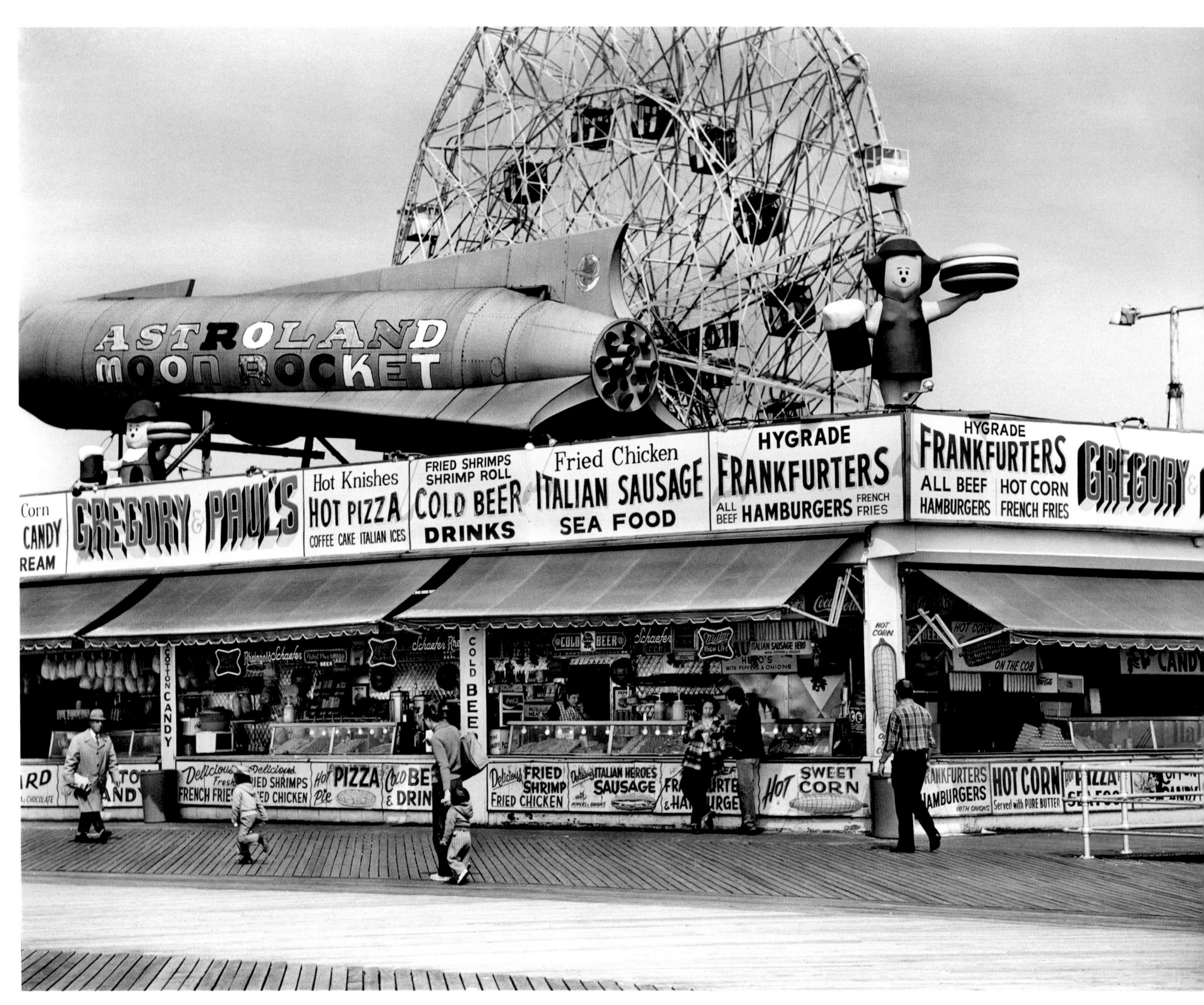

ASTROLAND MOON ROCKET
Corn
CANDY
REAM
GREGORY & PAUL'S
Hot Knishes
HOT PIZZA
COFFEE CAKE ITALIAN ICES
FRIED SHRIMPS
SHRIMP ROLL
COLD BEER
DRINKS
Fried Chicken
ITALIAN SAUSAGE
SEA FOOD
HYGRADE
FRANKFURTERS
ALL BEEF HAMBURGERS
FRENCH FRIES
HYGRADE
FRANKFURTERS
ALL BEEF HAMBURGERS
HOT CORN
FRENCH FRIES
GREGORY &
COTTON CANDY
COLD BEER
HOT CORN
ON THE COB
Delicious
Fresh
FRENCH FRIES
Delicious
FRIED SHRIMPS
FRIED CHICKEN
Hot
PIZZA
Pie
Cold BEER
& DRINKS
Delicious
FRIED
SHRIMP
FRIED CHICKEN
Delicious ITALIAN HEROE'S
SAUSAGE
FRANKFURTERS
& HAMBURGERS
HOT
SWEET
CORN
FRANKFURTERS
HAMBURGERS
HOT CORN
Served with PURE BUTTER

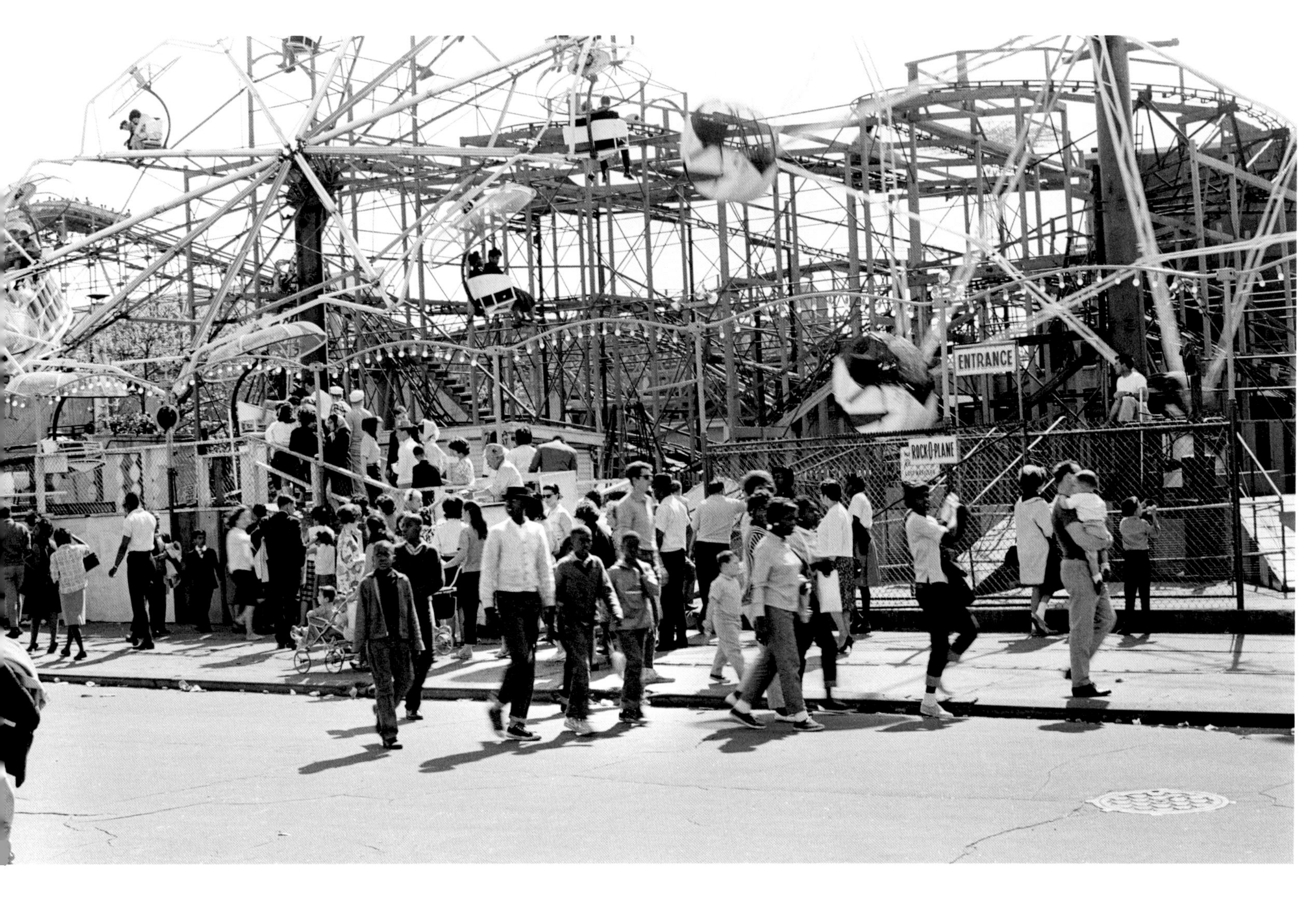

ENTRANCE
ROCK-O-PLANE

FORT GREENE · CLINTON HILL · BEDFORD-STUYVESANT
DOWNTOWN BROOKLYN

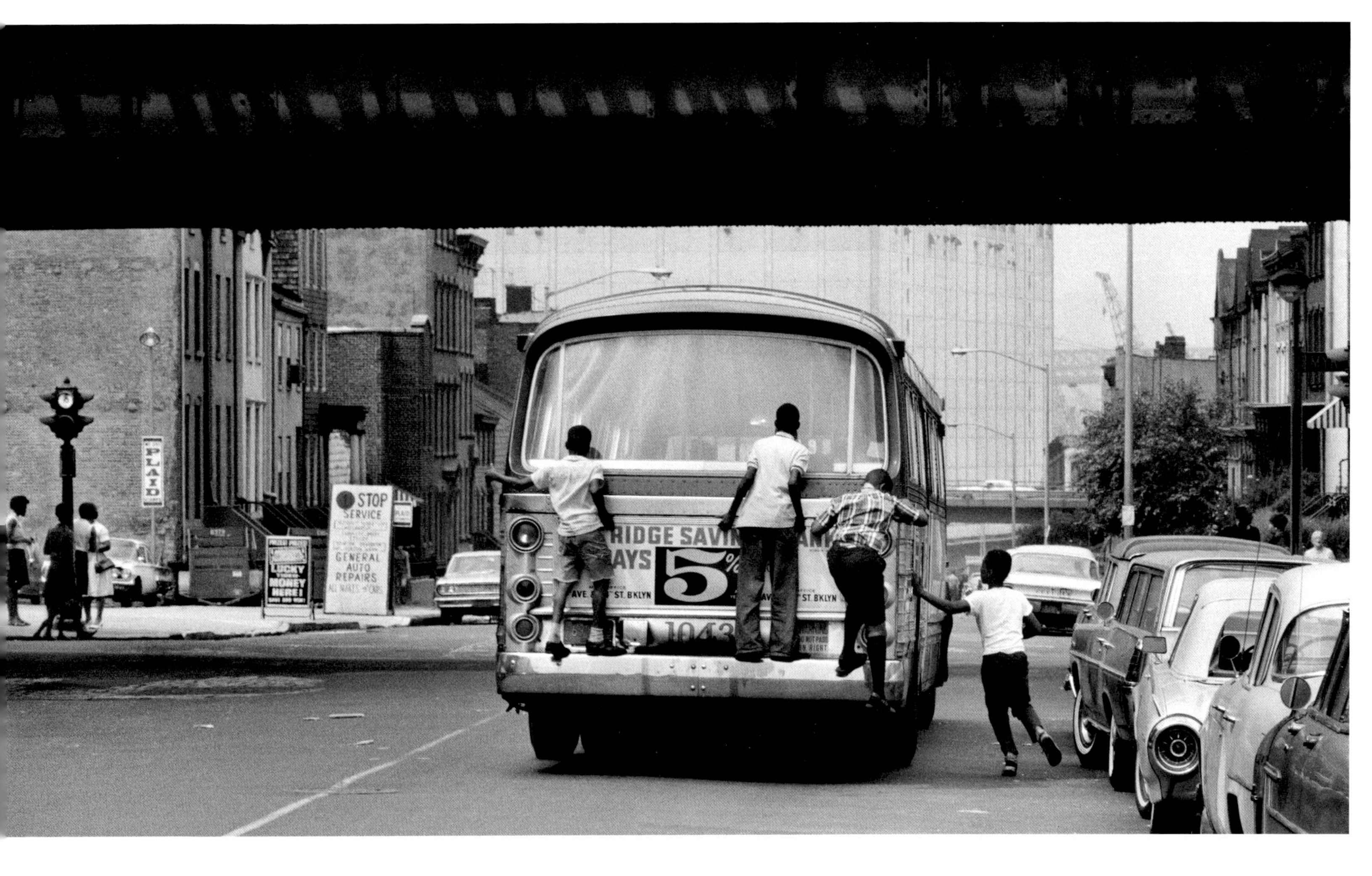
STOP
SERVICE
GENERAL
AUTO
REPAIRS
PLAID
LUCKY
MONEY
HERE!
RIDGE SAVINGS
AYS 5%
1043

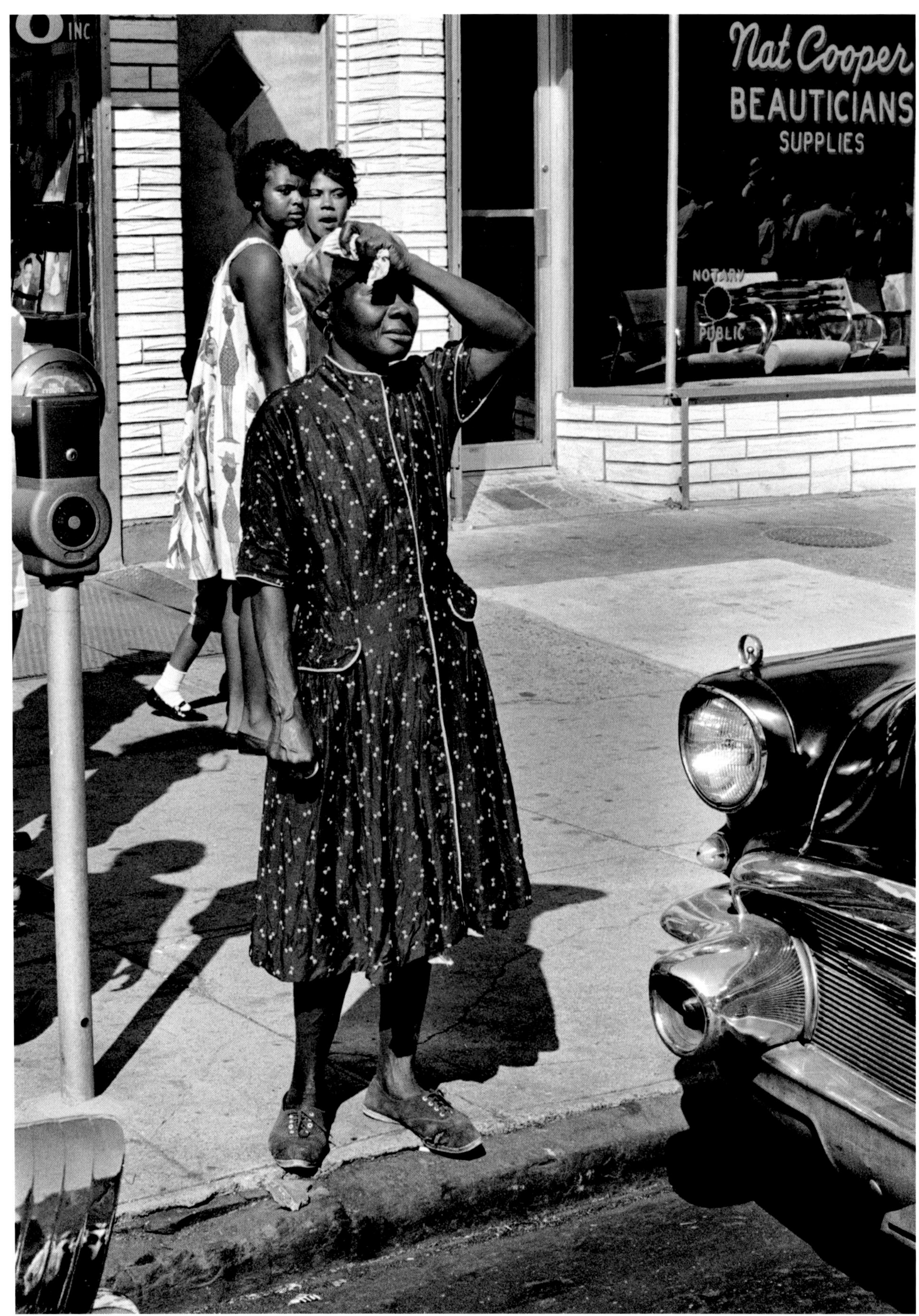

Nat Cooper
BEAUTICIANS
SUPPLIES
NOTARY
PUBLIC
INC.

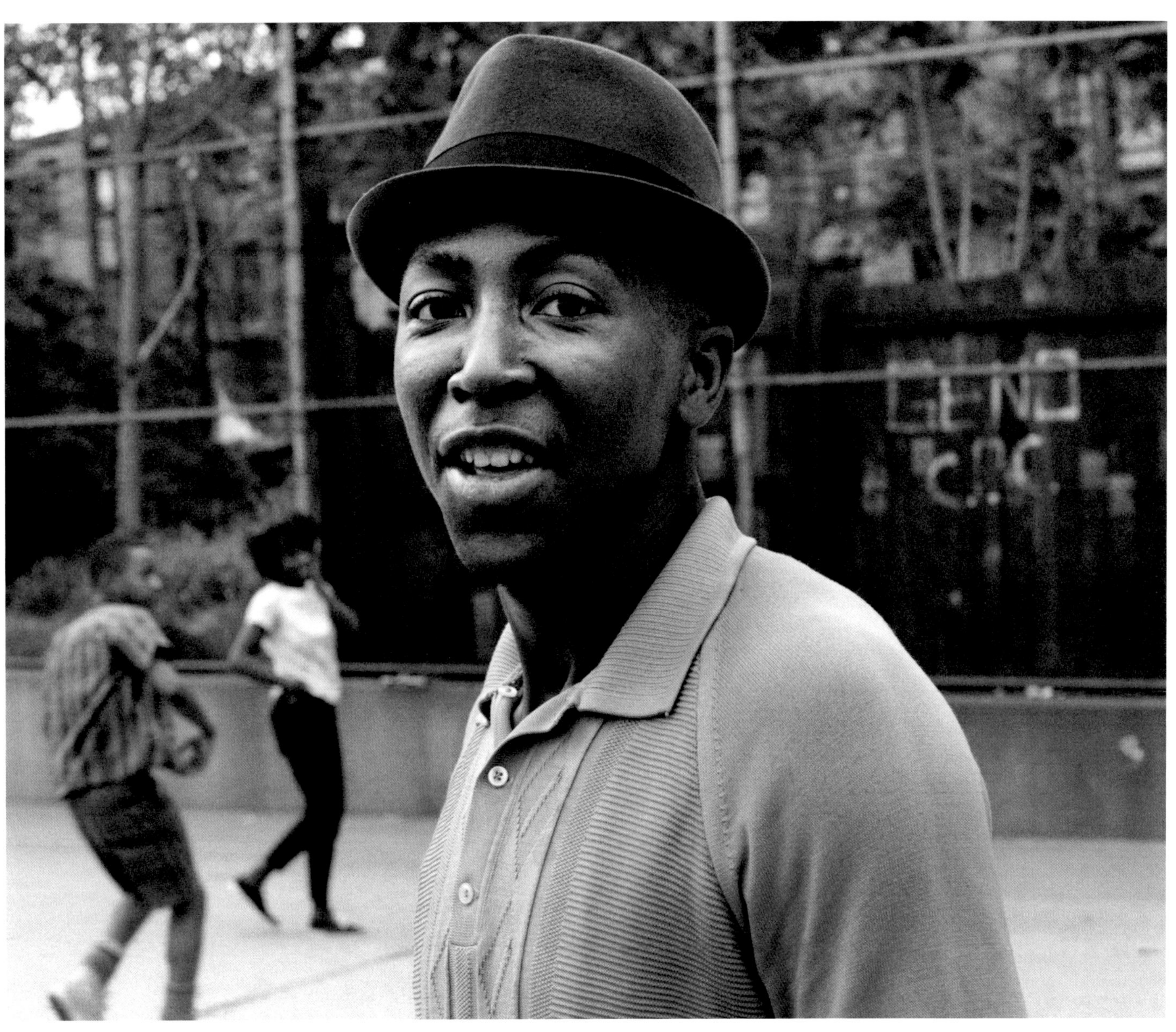

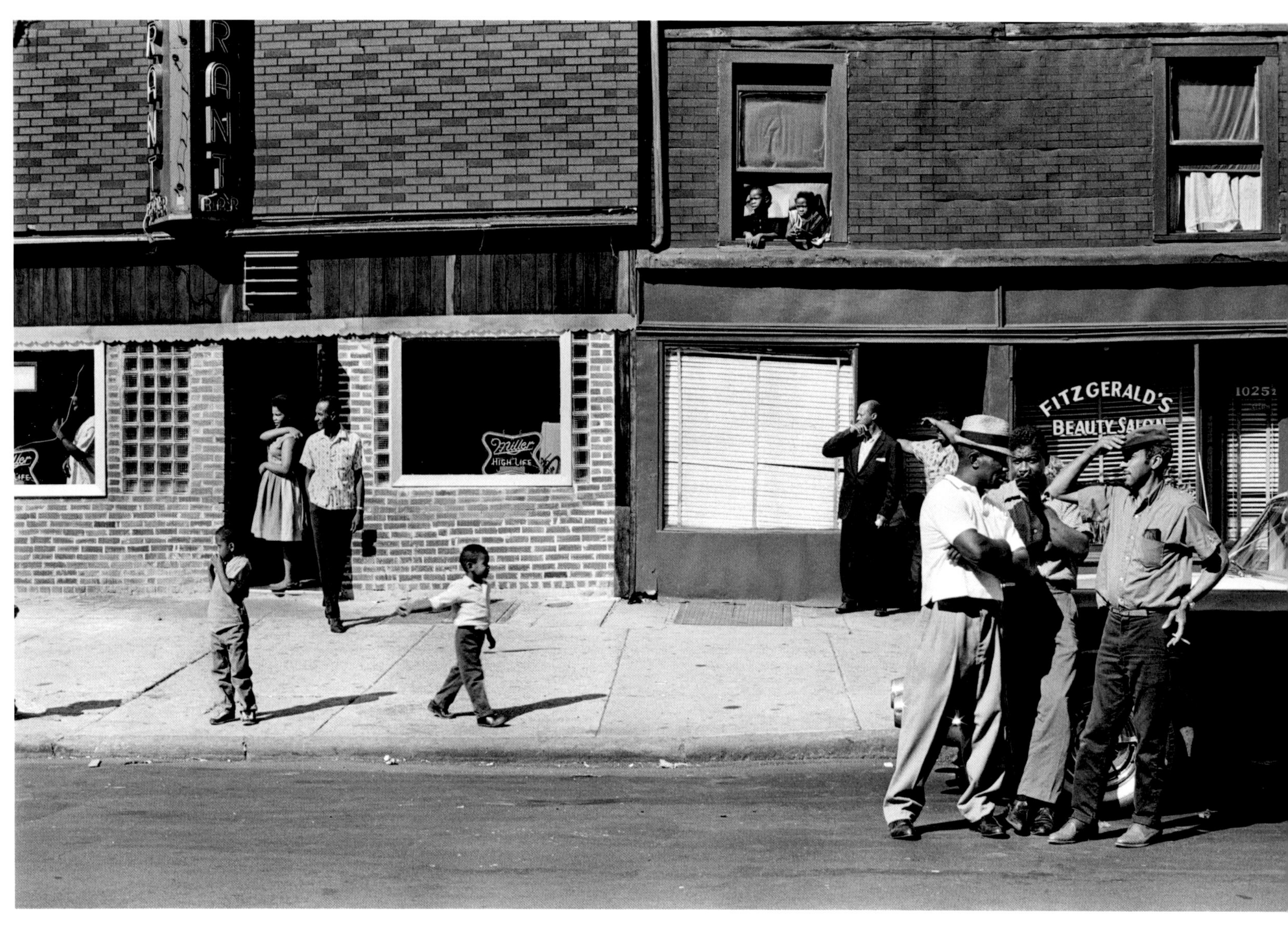

FITZGERALD'S
BEAUTY SALON
1025½
Miller
HIGH LIFE

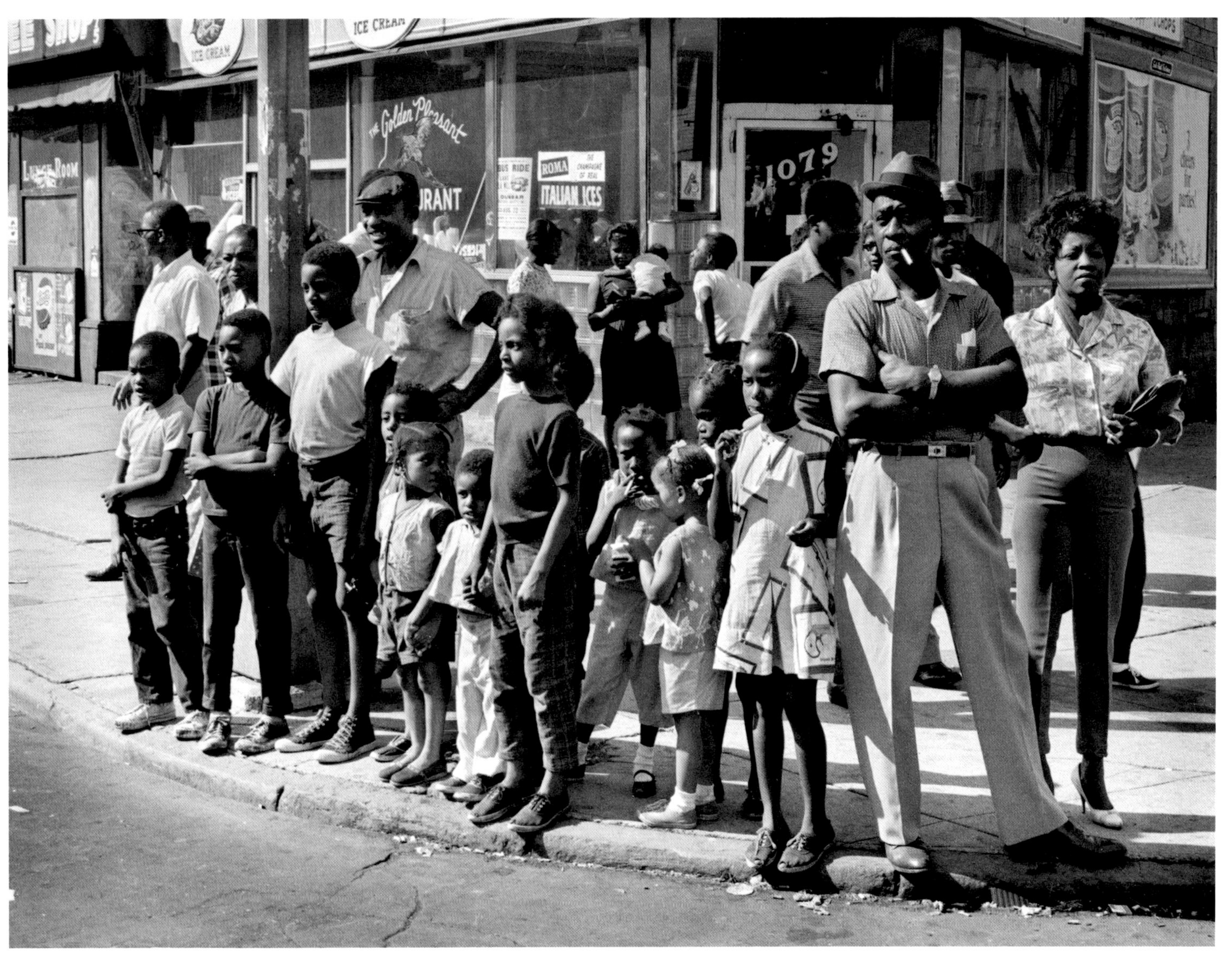

ICE CREAM
The Golden Pheasant
RESTAURANT
ROMA
ITALIAN ICES
1079

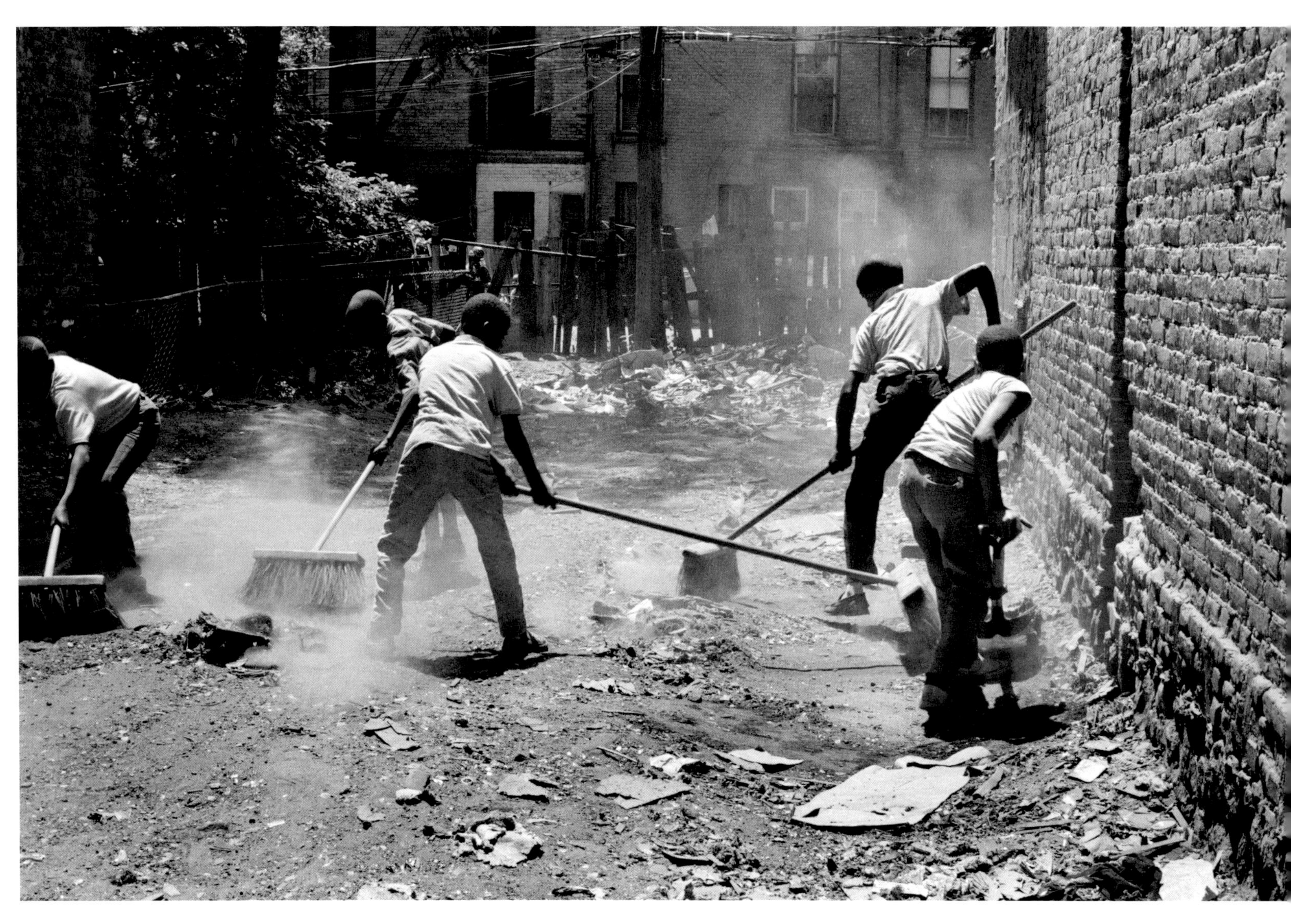

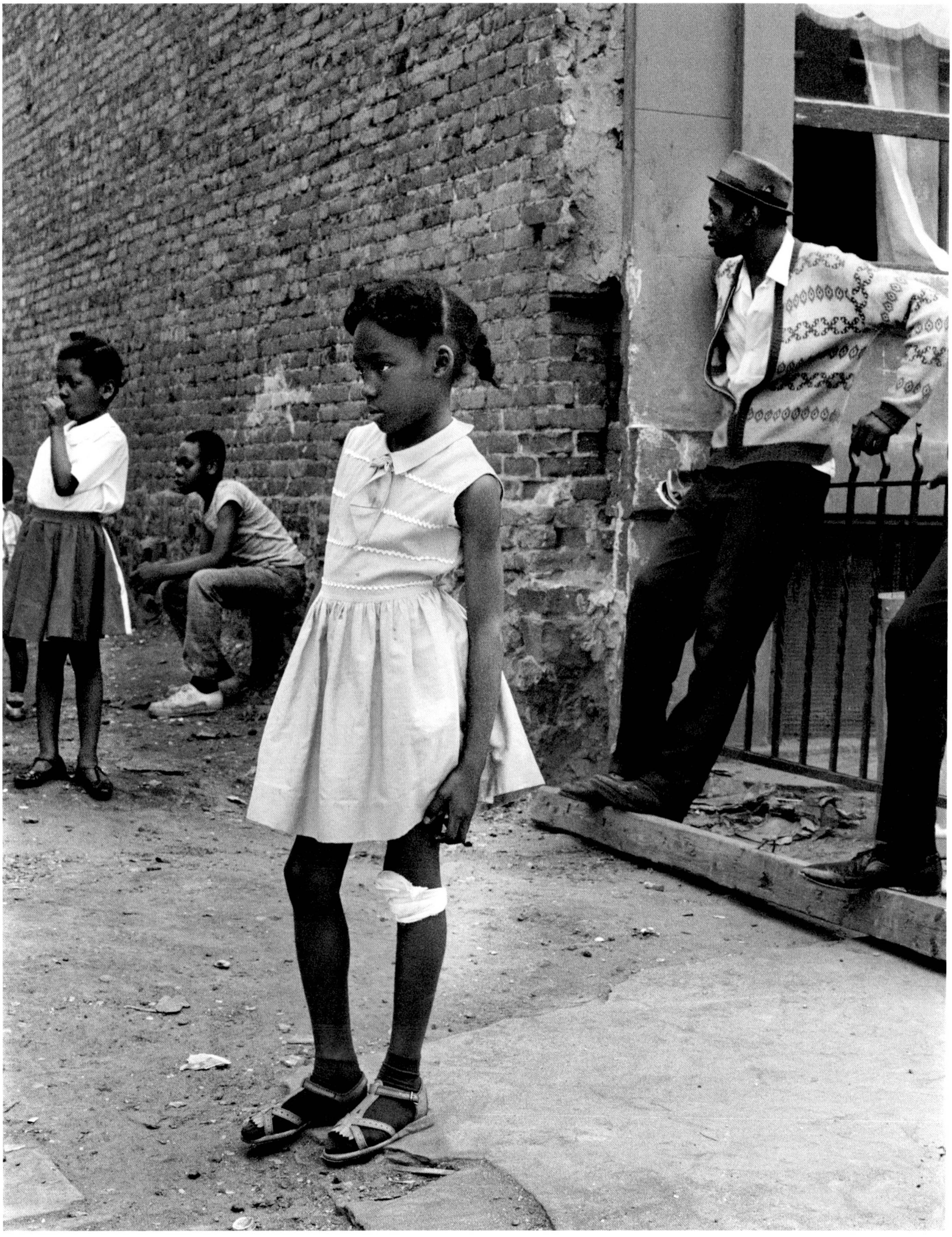

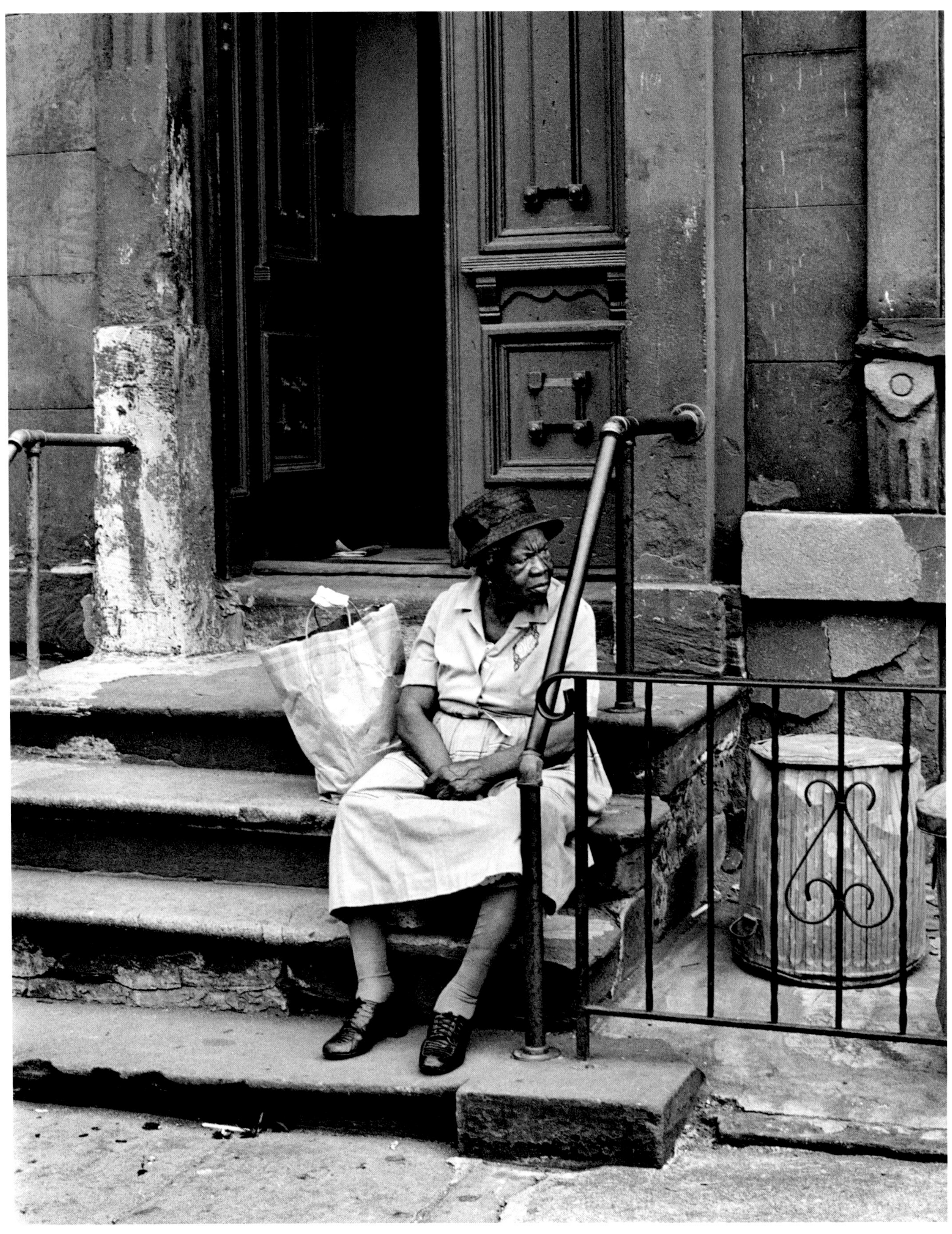

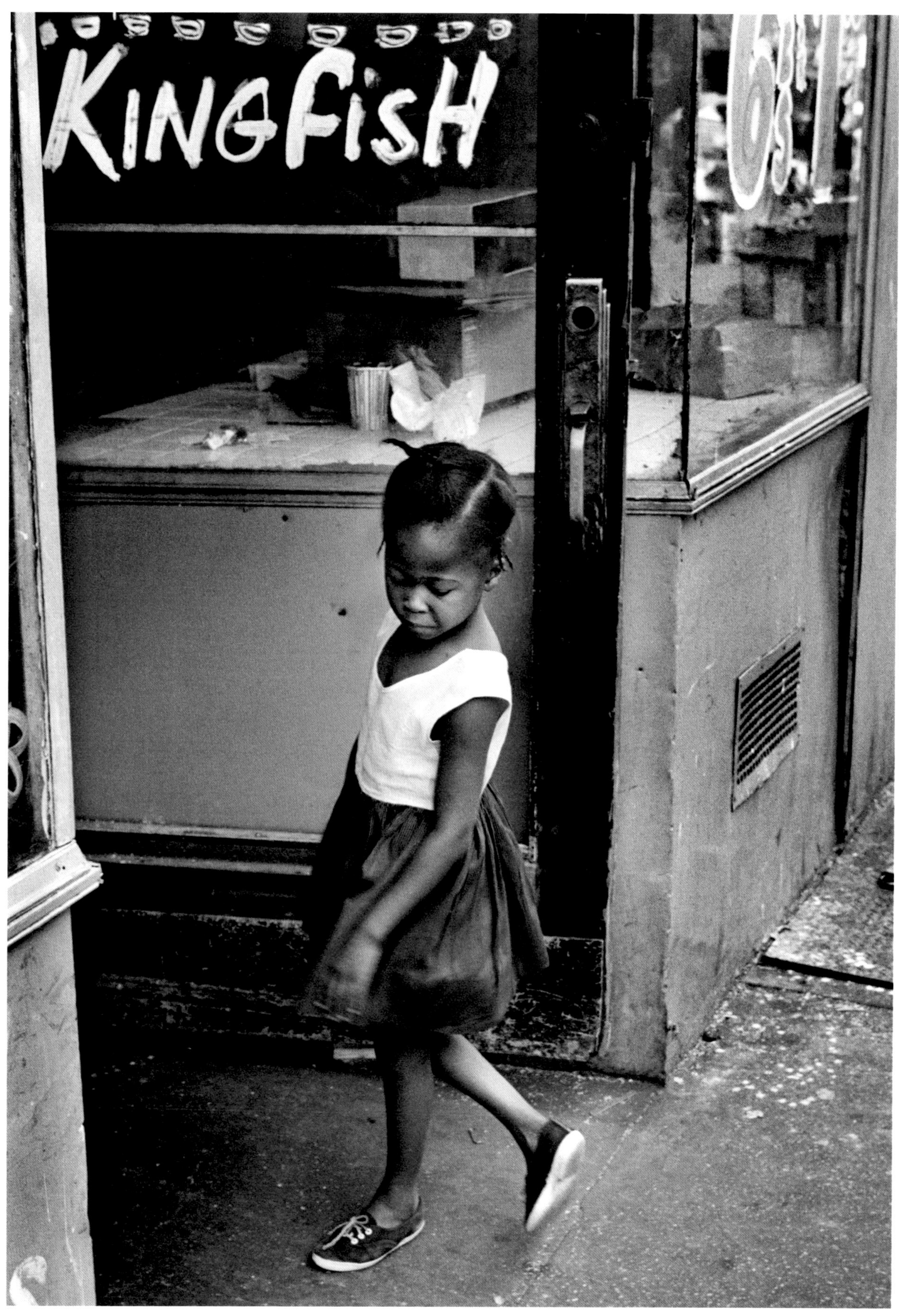

KINGFiSH

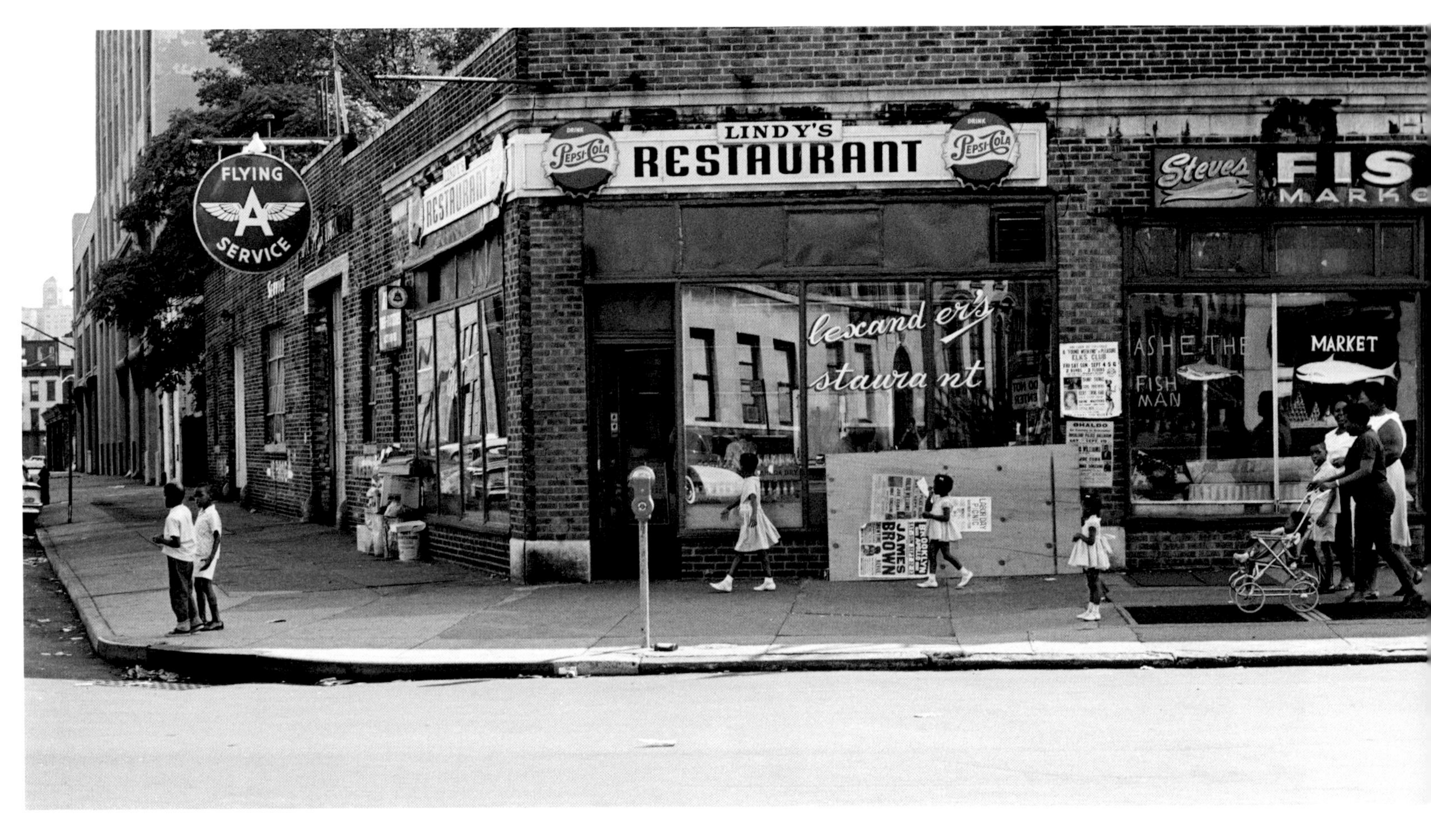

FLYING
A
SERVICE
LINDY'S
RESTAURANT
DRINK Pepsi-Cola
DRINK Pepsi-Cola
lexand er's
staura nt
Steves
FISH
MARKET
ASHE THE
FISH MAN
MARKET
JAMES BROWN

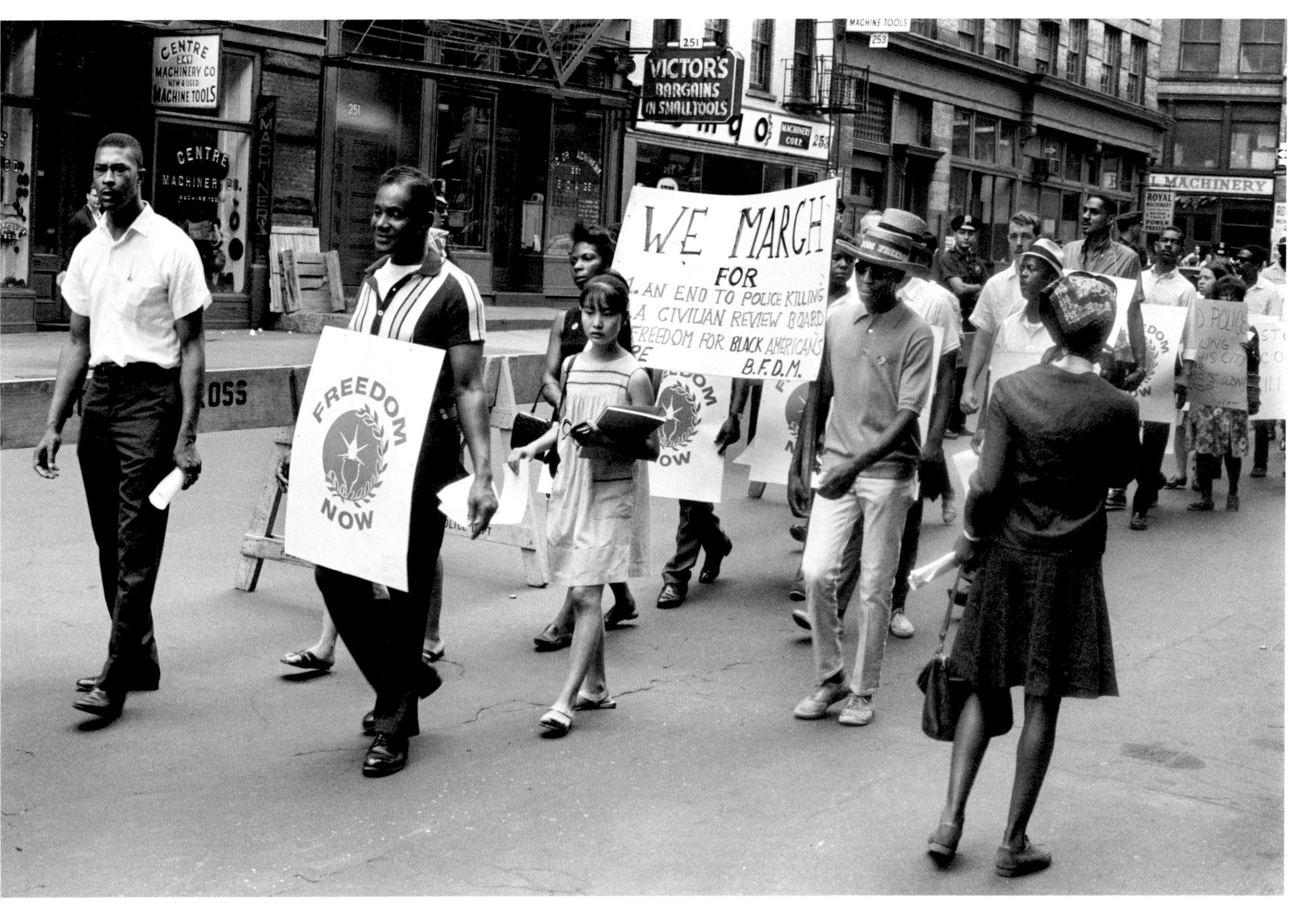
CENTRE
MACHINERY CO
NEW & USED
MACHINE TOOLS
VICTOR'S
BARGAINS
IN SMALL TOOLS
MACHINE TOOLS
ROYAL
MACHINERY
FREEDOM
NOW
WE MARCH
FOR
1. AN END TO POLICE KILLINGS
2. A CIVILIAN REVIEW BOARD
3. FREEDOM FOR BLACK AMERICANS
B.F.D.M.

It was a late Friday afternoon in July. Having just finished photographing on Gates Avenue between Vanderbilt and Clinton Avenues, I was on my way home, walking to Clinton Avenue, when I saw these fellows—I think they had come out of a tenement building on Clinton, and were headed towards me. (A year-and-a-half earlier, I had moved into this multiracial and multi-class neighborhood on Clinton Avenue, and became a recreation leader in the nearby P.S. 20 playground, in Fort Greene, where another youth group, the Cross Park Chaplains, hung out.) I would bring my camera to photograph there periodically. I had not been aware that some of the Medallion Lords also hung out there, and that the two groups were friendly. As they got nearer, I wanted very much to photograph them, but wondered, "How in the world can I approach these teenagers to make a photograph?" All of a sudden, one of the guys yelled out, "Hey Parkee, take our picture!"

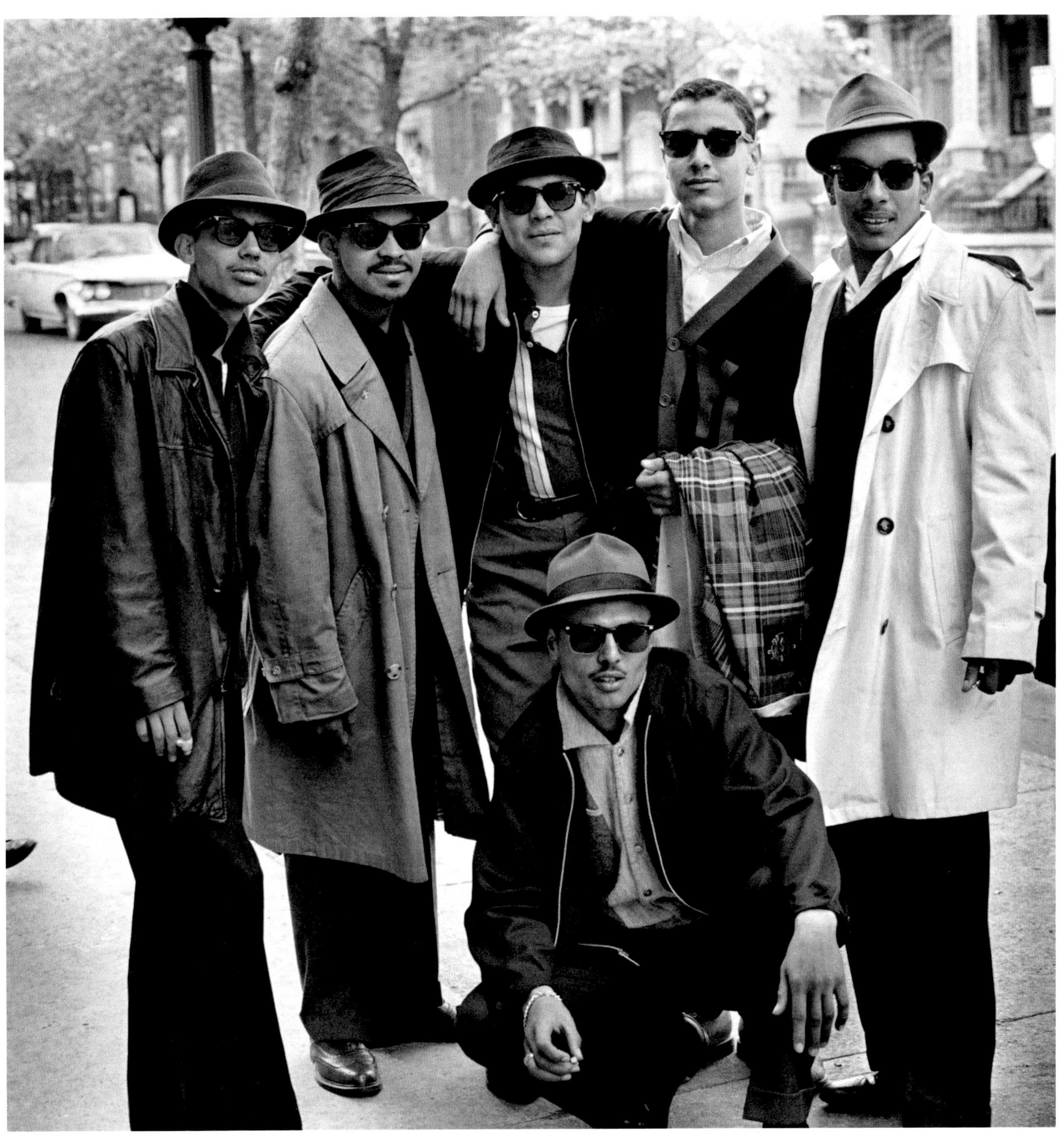

NO WAR

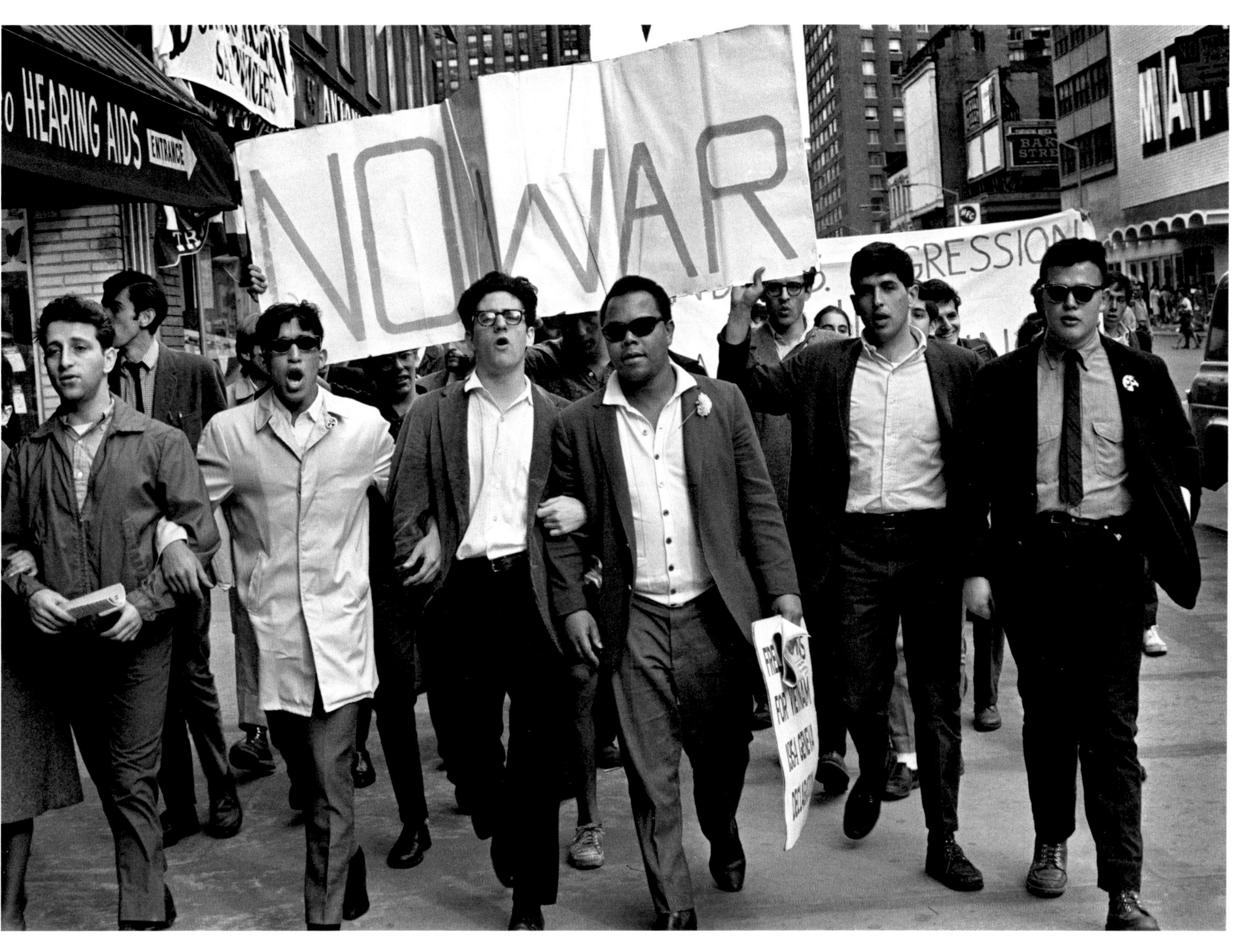

HEARING AIDS
ENTRANCE
SERVICES
NO WAR
GRESSION
BAKER STREET

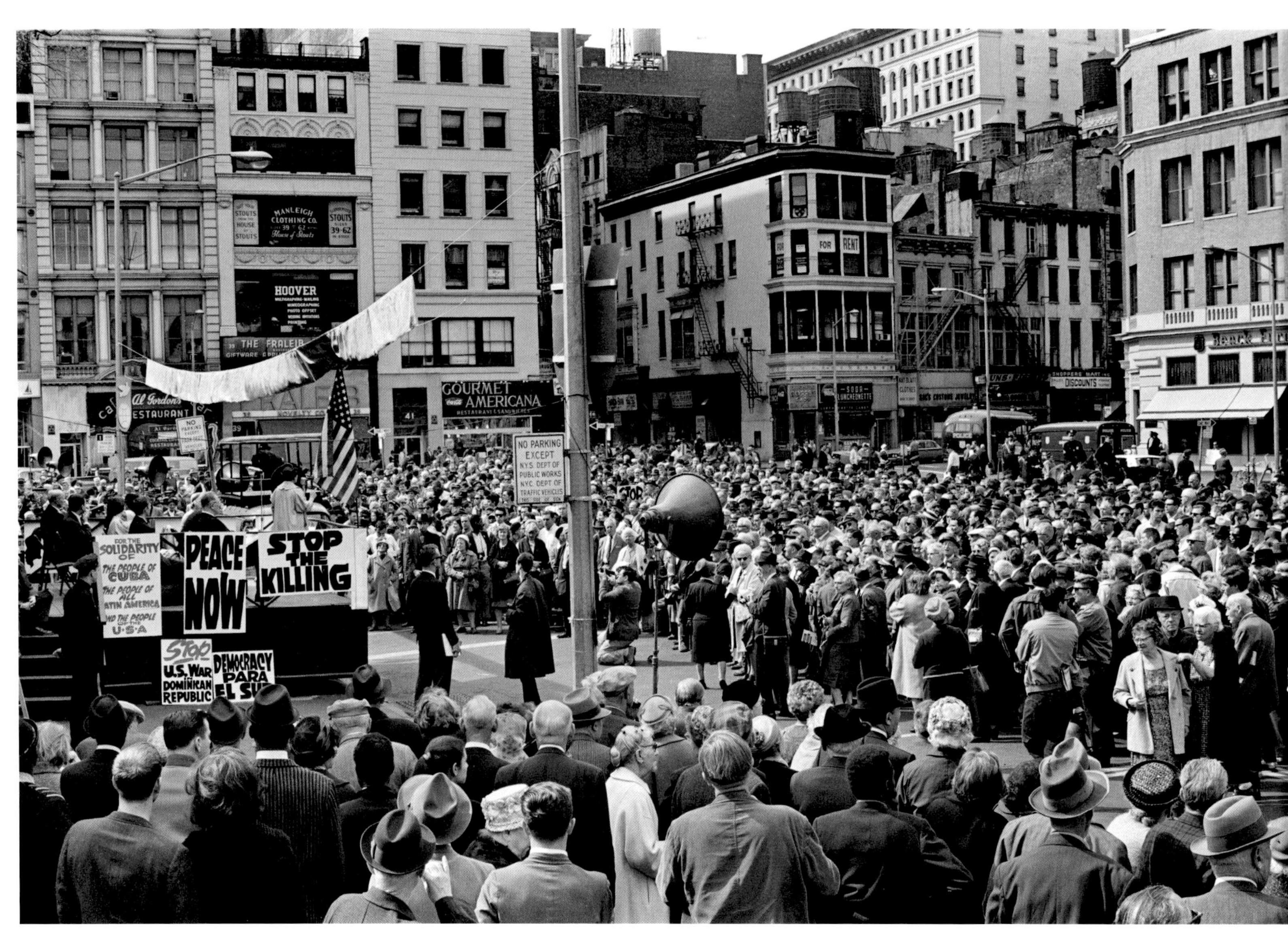

FOR THE
SOLIDARITY
OF
THE PEOPLE OF
CUBA
THE PEOPLE OF ALL
LATIN AMERICA
AND THE PEOPLE
OF THE
U·S·A
PEACE
NOW
STOP
THE
KILLING
STOP
U.S. WAR
DOMINICAN
REPUBLIC
DEMOCRACY
PARA
EL SUR
MANLEIGH
CLOTHING CO.
HOOVER
GOURMET
AMERICANA
NO PARKING
EXCEPT
N.Y.S. DEPT OF
PUBLIC WORKS
N.Y.C. DEPT OF
TRAFFIC VEHICLES
FOR RENT
DISCOUNTS

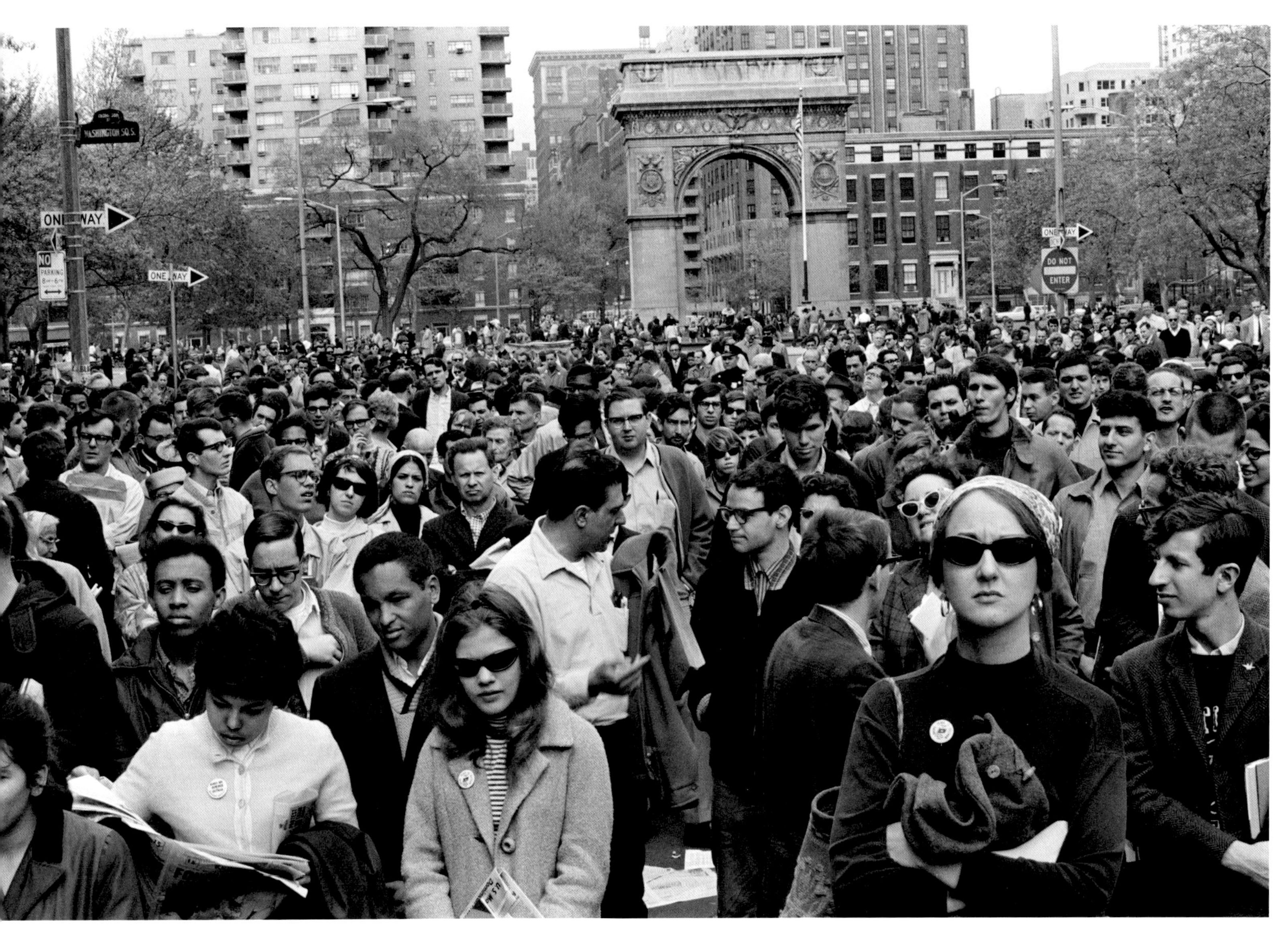

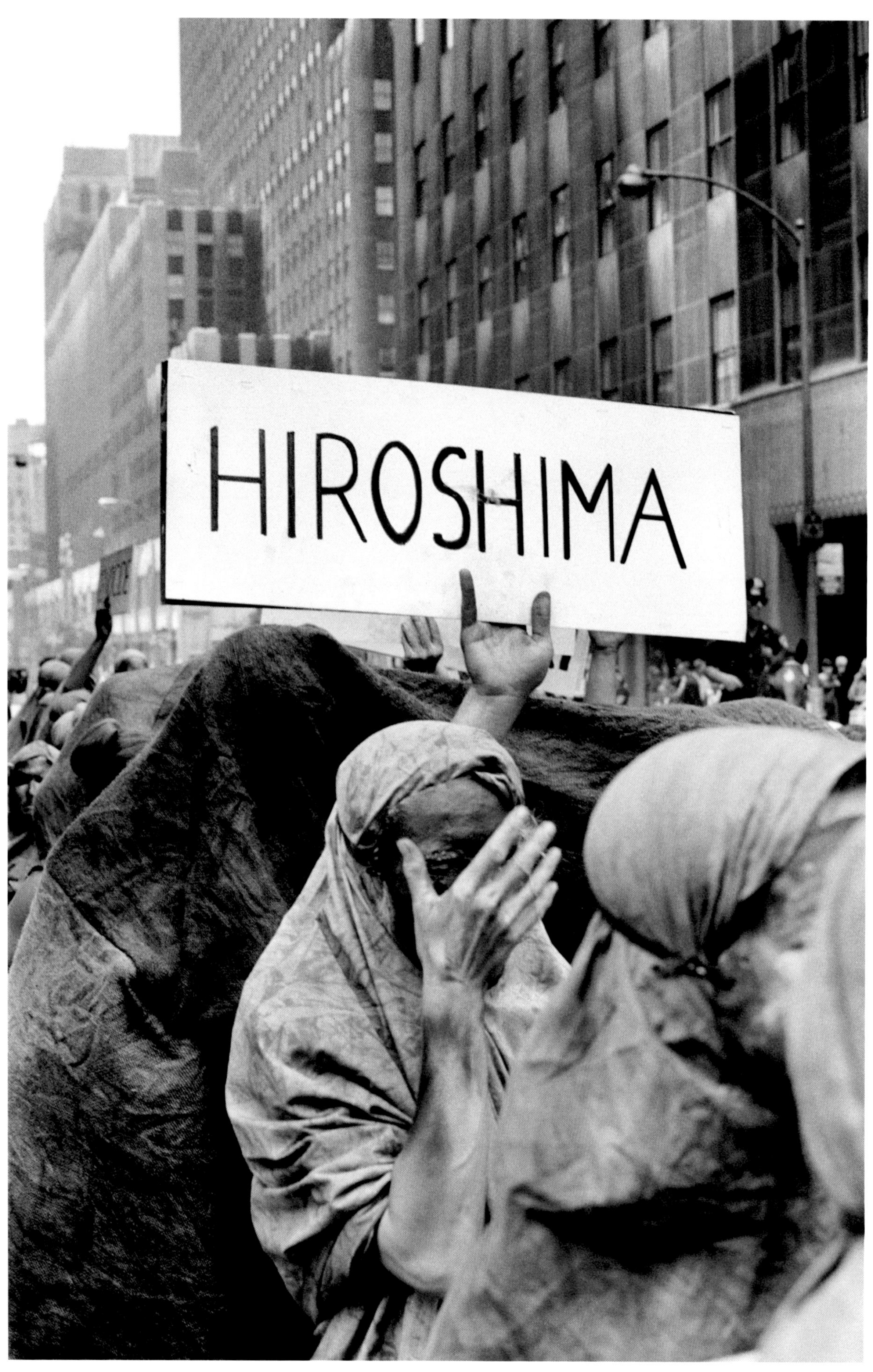

HIROSHIMA

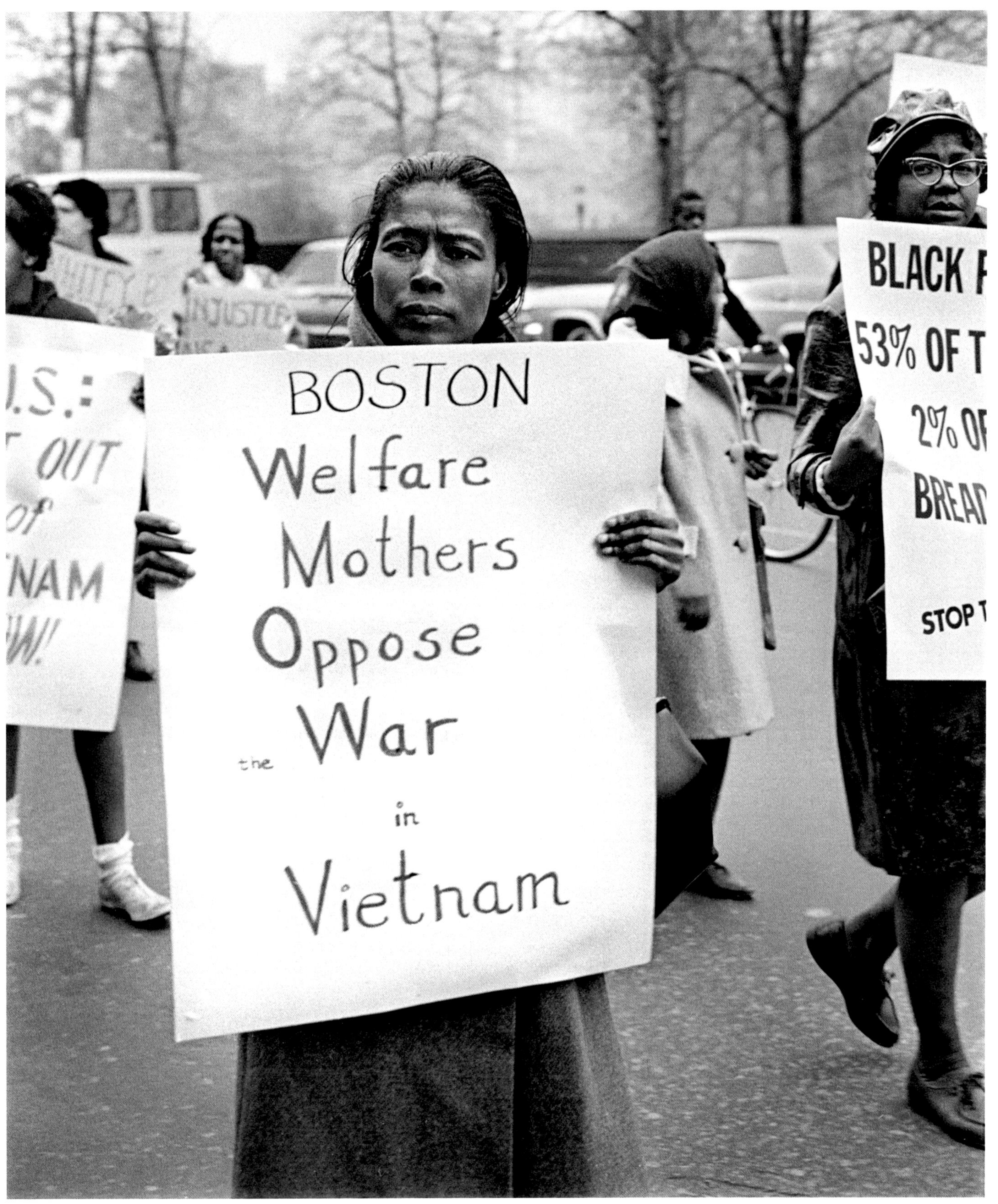
BOSTON
Welfare
Mothers
Oppose
the War
in
Vietnam
U.S.:
OUT
of
VIETNAM
NOW!
BLACK
53% OF T
2% OF
BREAD
STOP T

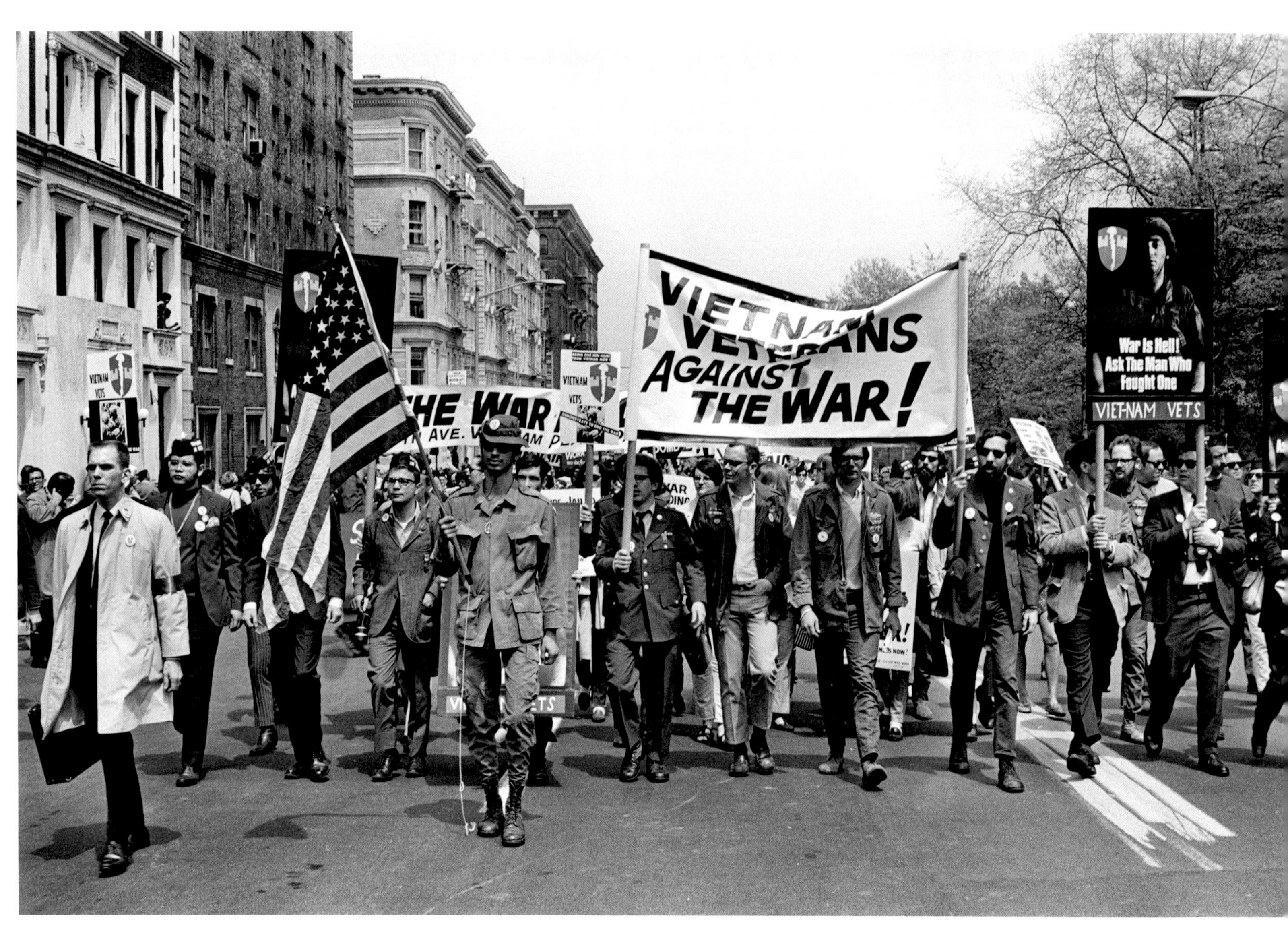
VIET NAM VETERANS AGAINST THE WAR!
THE WAR
War Is Hell !
Ask The Man Who
Fought One
VIETNAM VETS
VIETNAM VETS
VIETNAM VETS

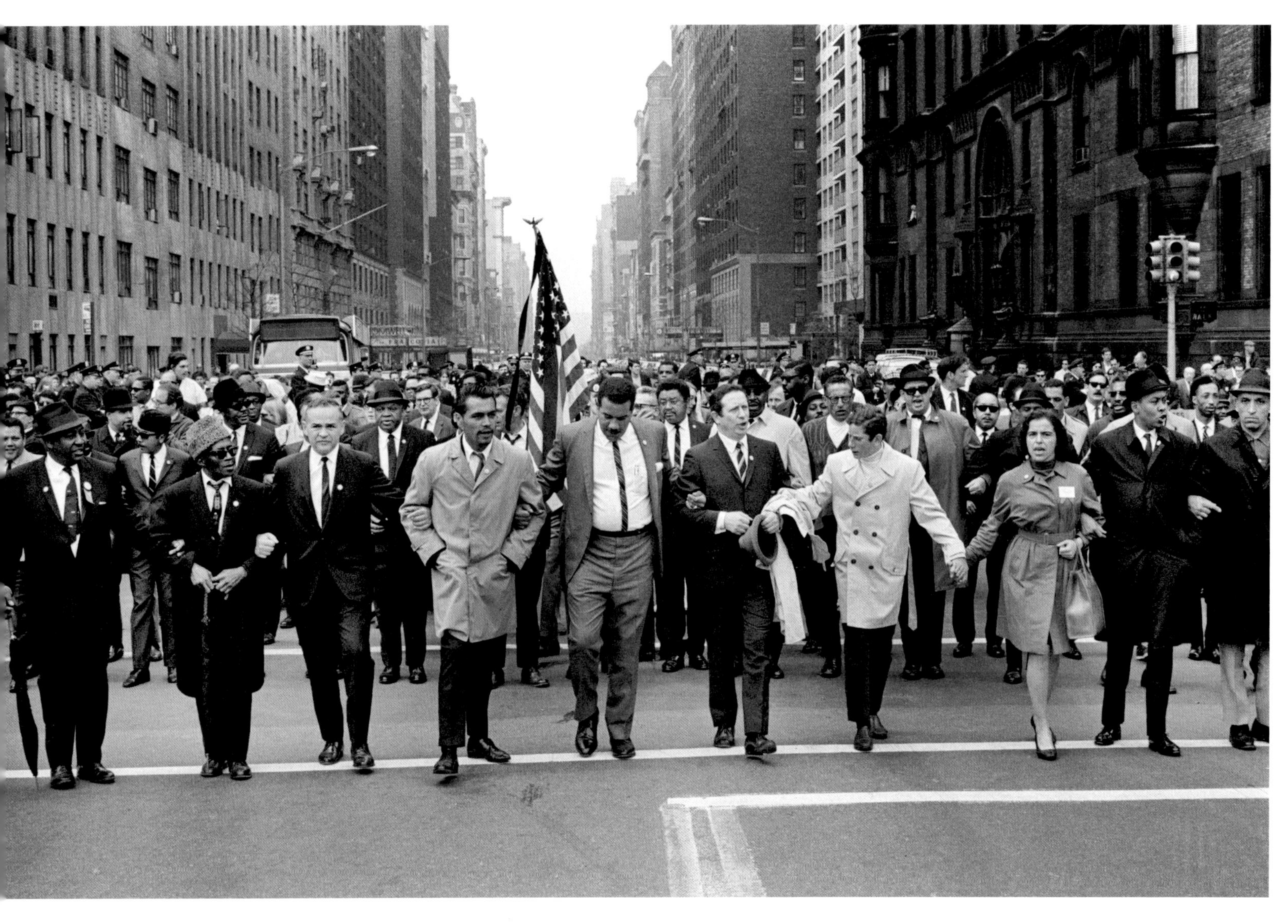

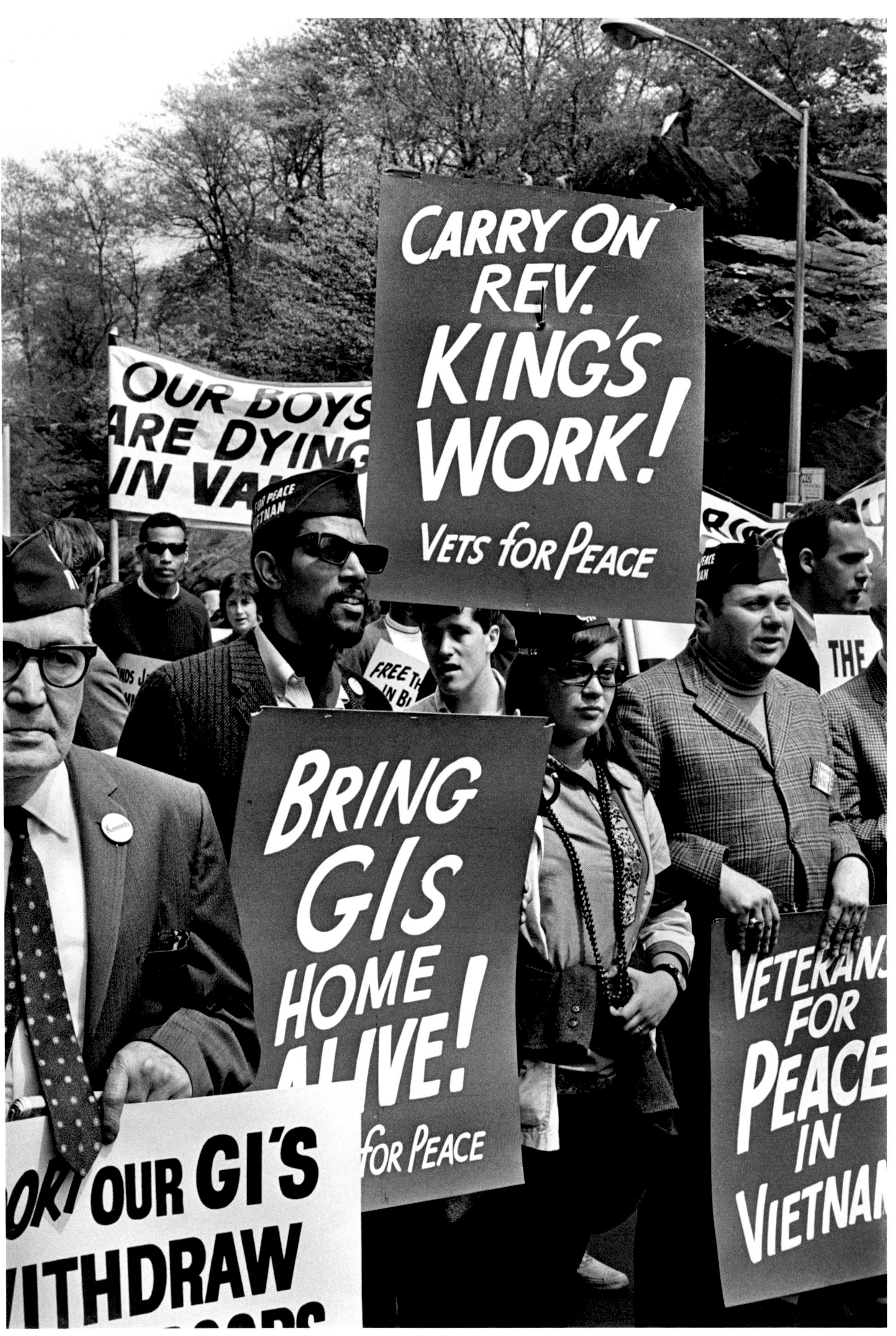
CARRY ON REV. KING'S WORK!
VETS FOR PEACE
OUR BOYS ARE DYING IN VA
BRING GIS HOME ALIVE!
for PEACE
VETERANS FOR PEACE IN VIETNAM
OUR GI'S WITHDRAW
THE

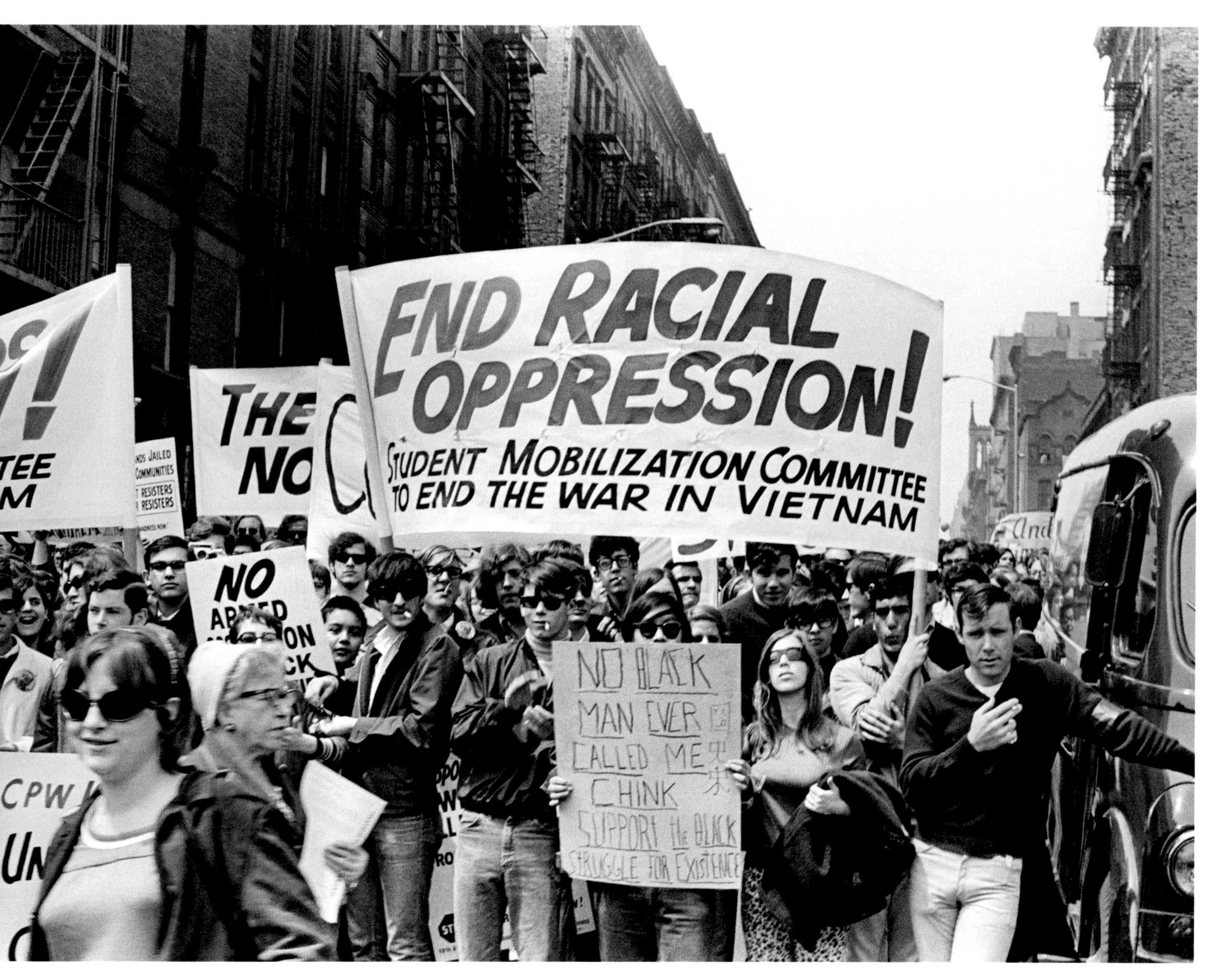

END RACIAL OPPRESSION!
STUDENT MOBILIZATION COMMITTEE TO END THE WAR IN VIETNAM
THE
NO
NO
NO BLACK MAN EVER CALLED ME CHINK SUPPORT the BLACK STRUGGLE FOR EXISTENCE
CPW

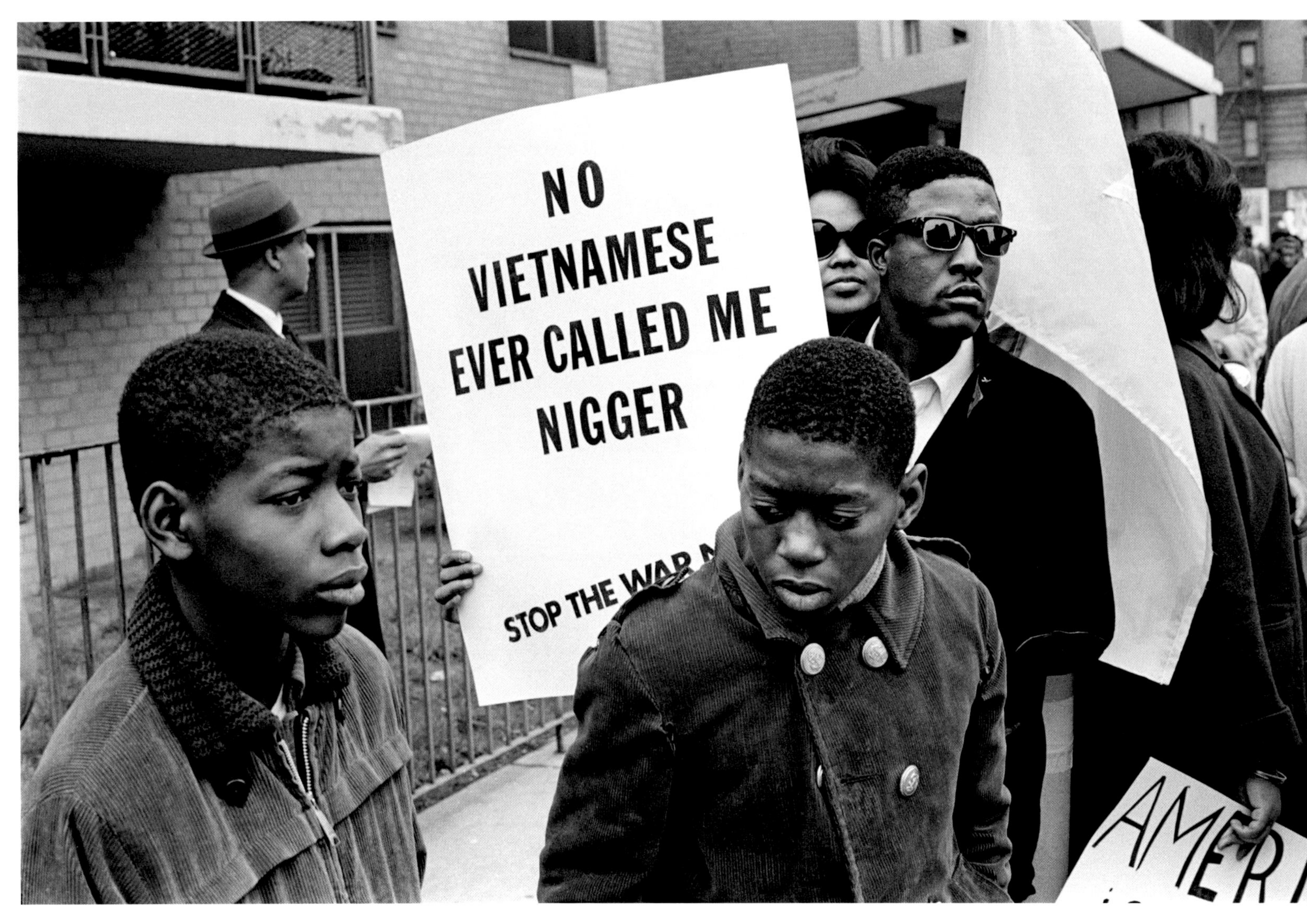
NO
VIETNAMESE
EVER CALLED ME
NIGGER
STOP THE WAR
AMER

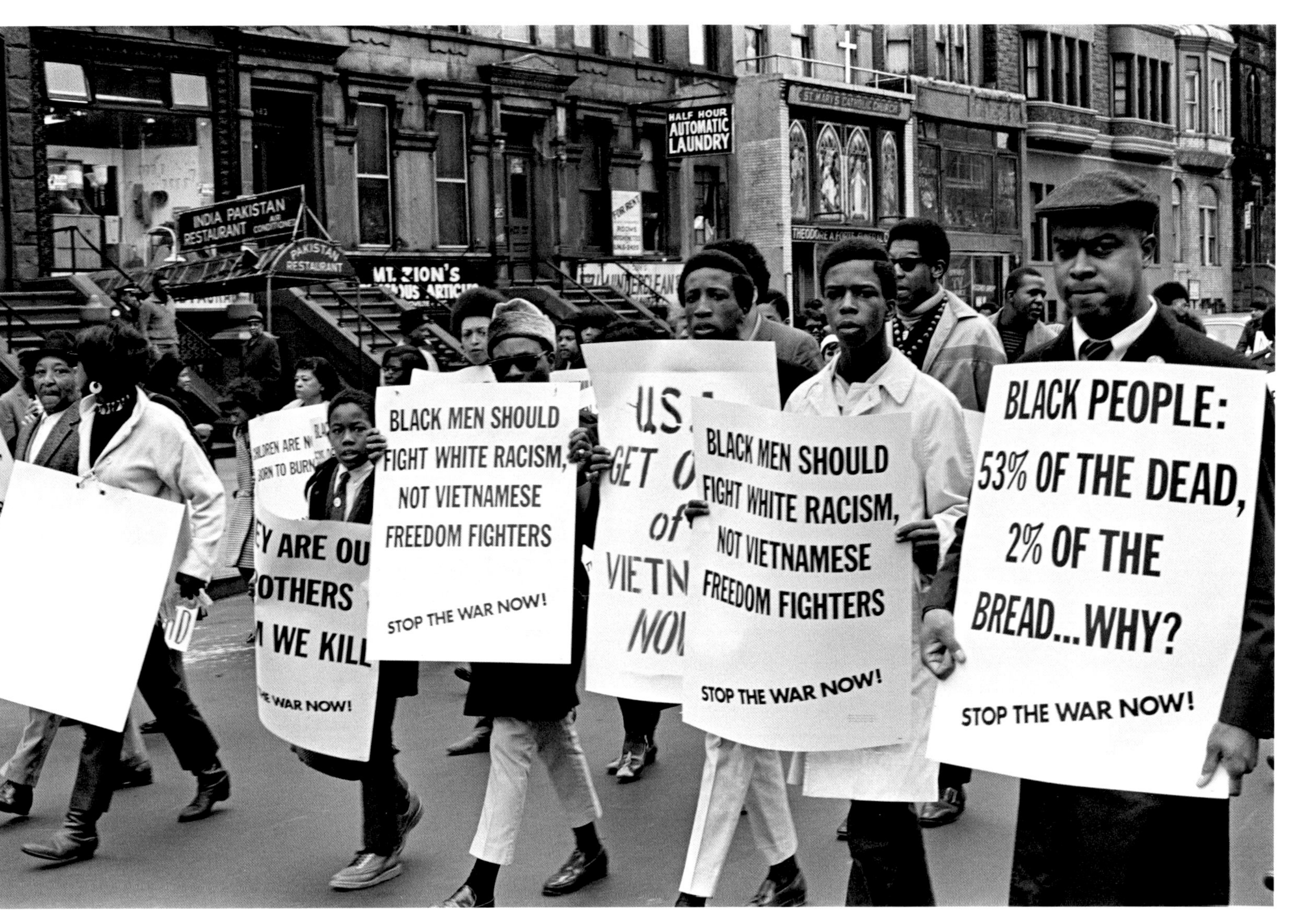
HALF HOUR
AUTOMATIC
LAUNDRY
INDIA PAKISTAN
RESTAURANT
PAKISTAN
RESTAURANT
MT. ZION'S
ST. MARY'S CATHOLIC CHURCH
BLACK MEN SHOULD
FIGHT WHITE RACISM,
NOT VIETNAMESE
FREEDOM FIGHTERS
STOP THE WAR NOW!
EY ARE OU
OTHERS
WE KILL
BLACK MEN SHOULD
FIGHT WHITE RACISM,
NOT VIETNAMESE
FREEDOM FIGHTERS
STOP THE WAR NOW!
U.S.
GET O
of
VIETN
NO
BLACK PEOPLE:
53% OF THE DEAD,
2% OF THE
BREAD...WHY?
STOP THE WAR NOW!

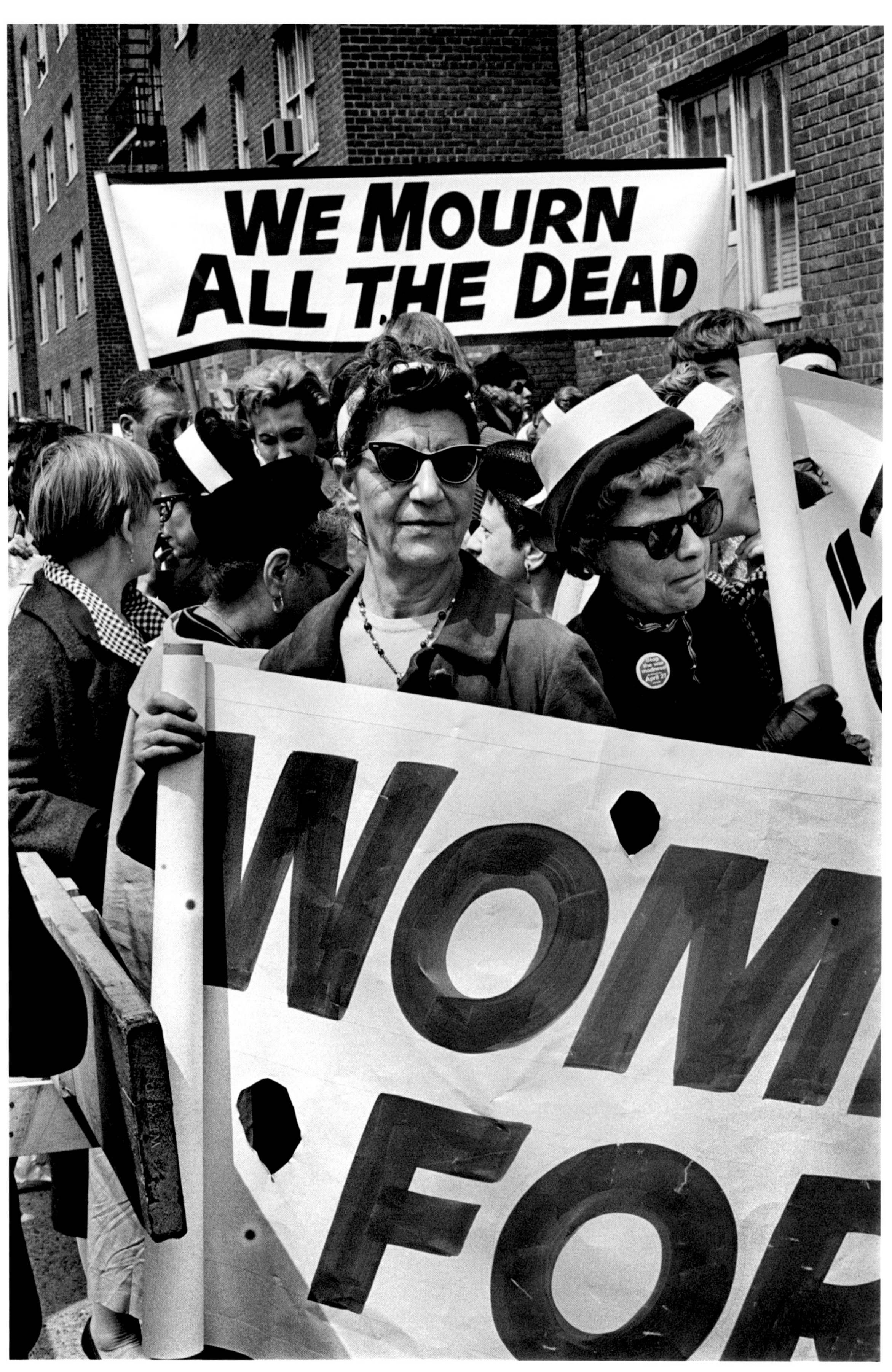

WE MOURN
ALL THE DEAD
WO
FOR

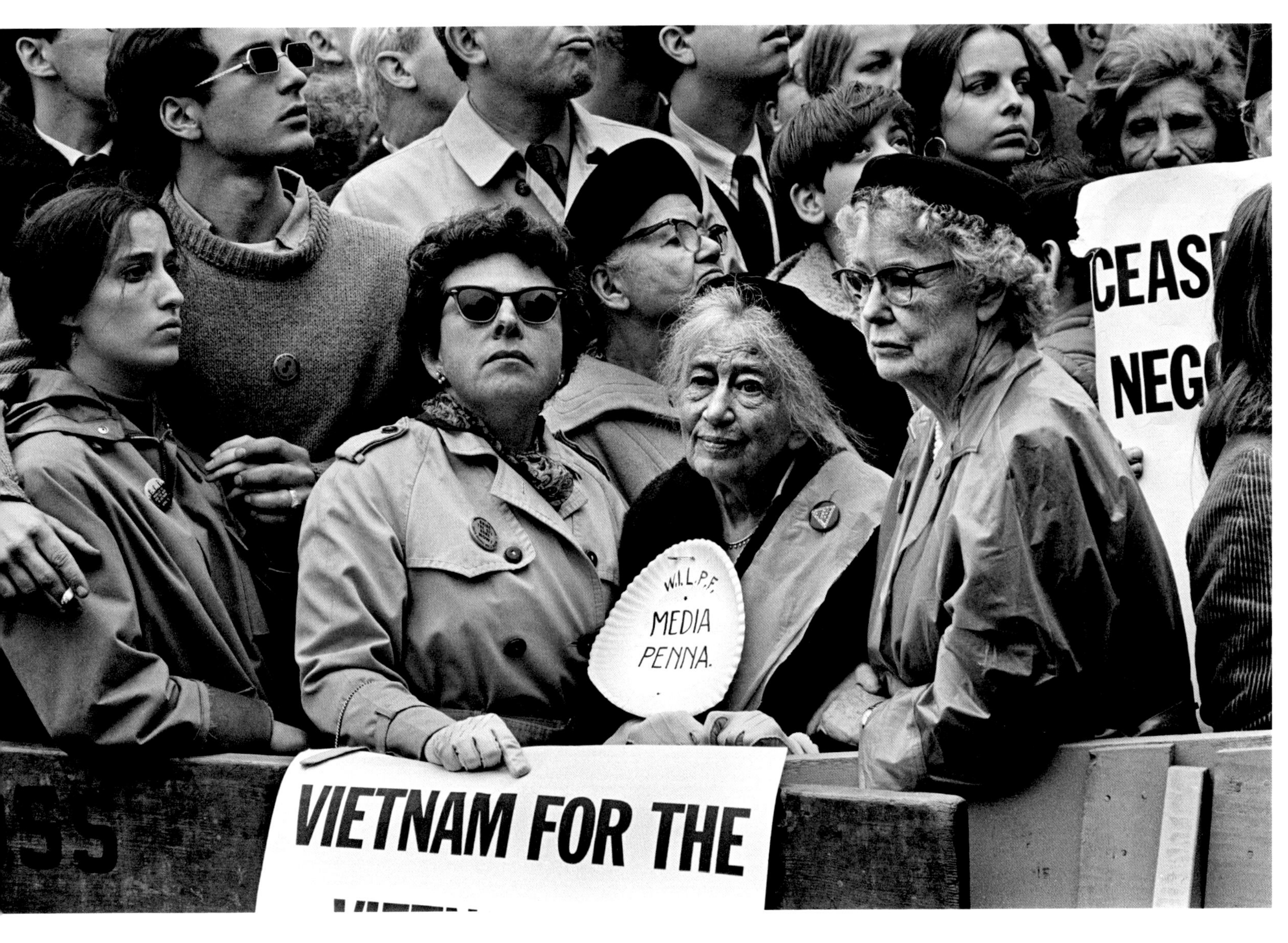

W.I.L.P.F.
MEDIA
PENNA.
VIETNAM FOR THE
CEASE
NEGO

DR. MARTIN LUTHER KING, JR.

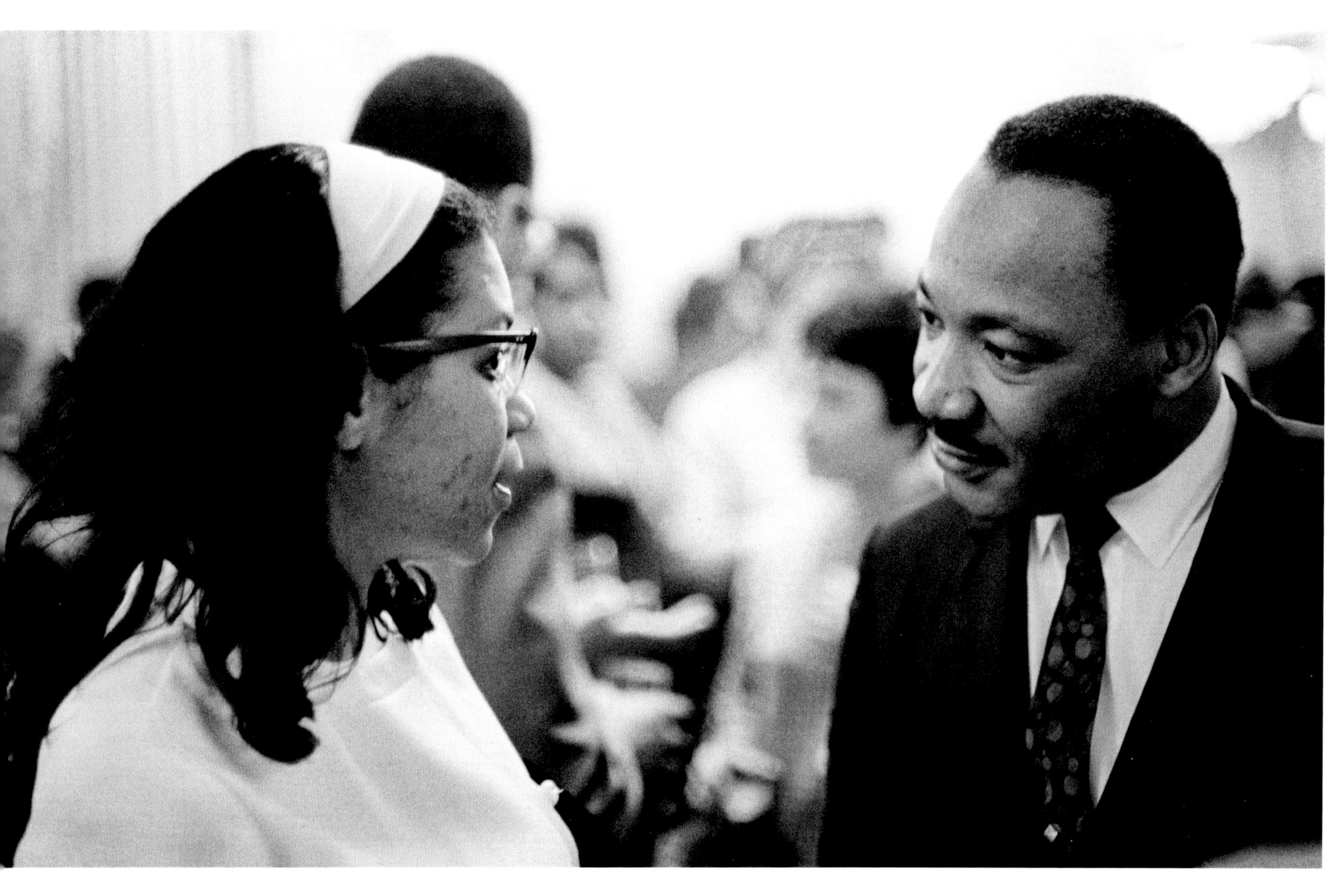

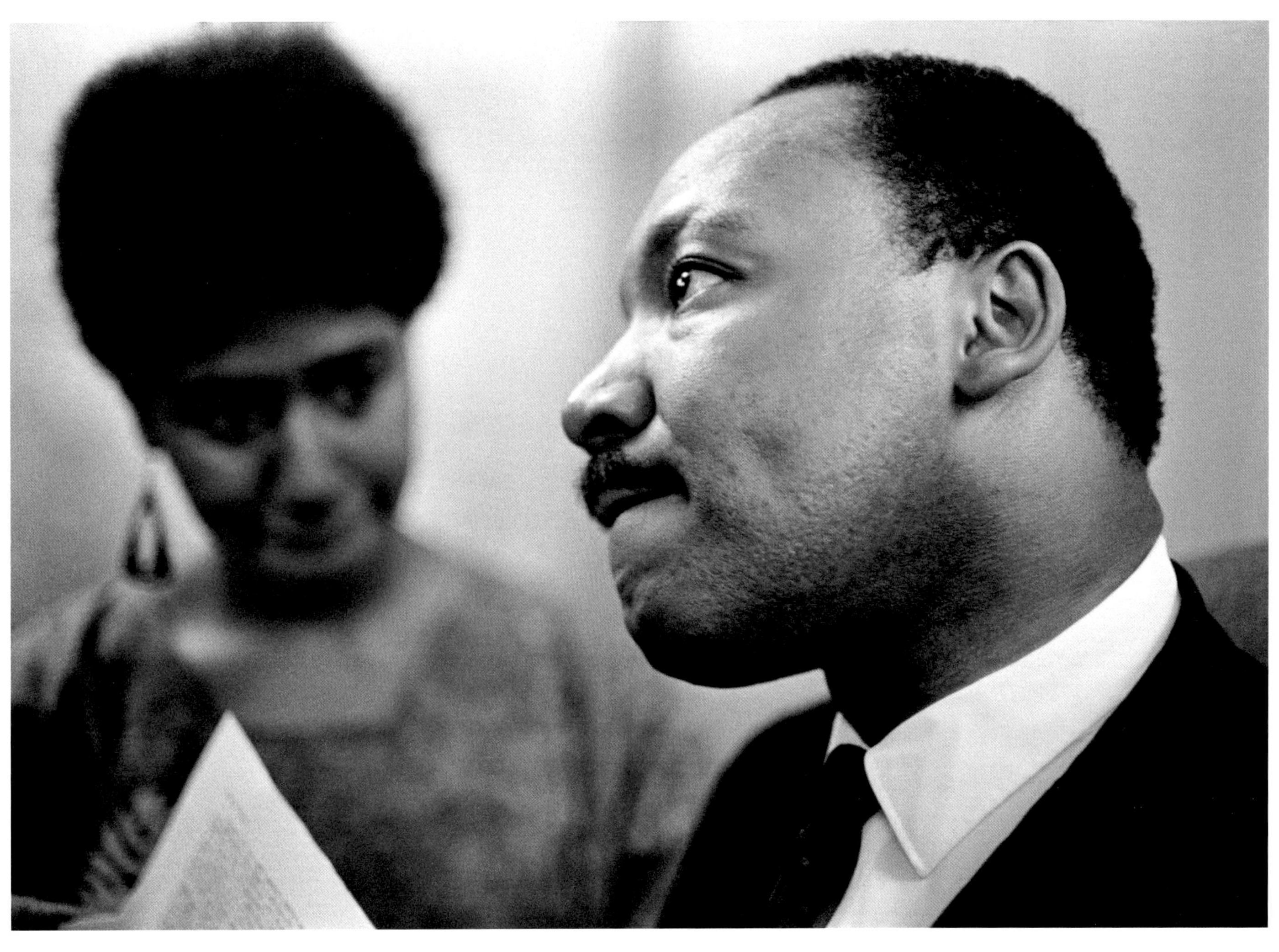

OCEAN HILL BROWNSVILLE

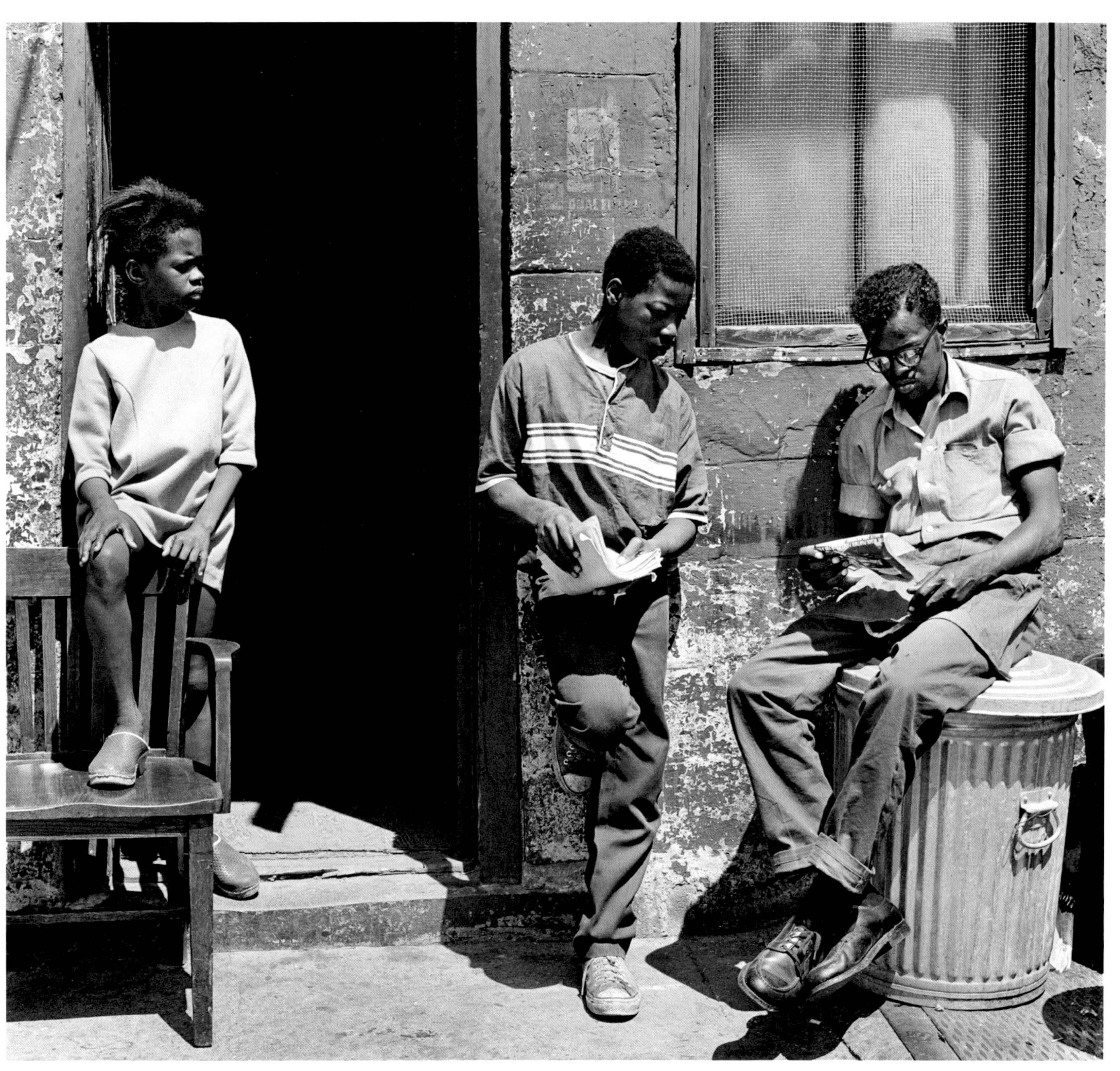

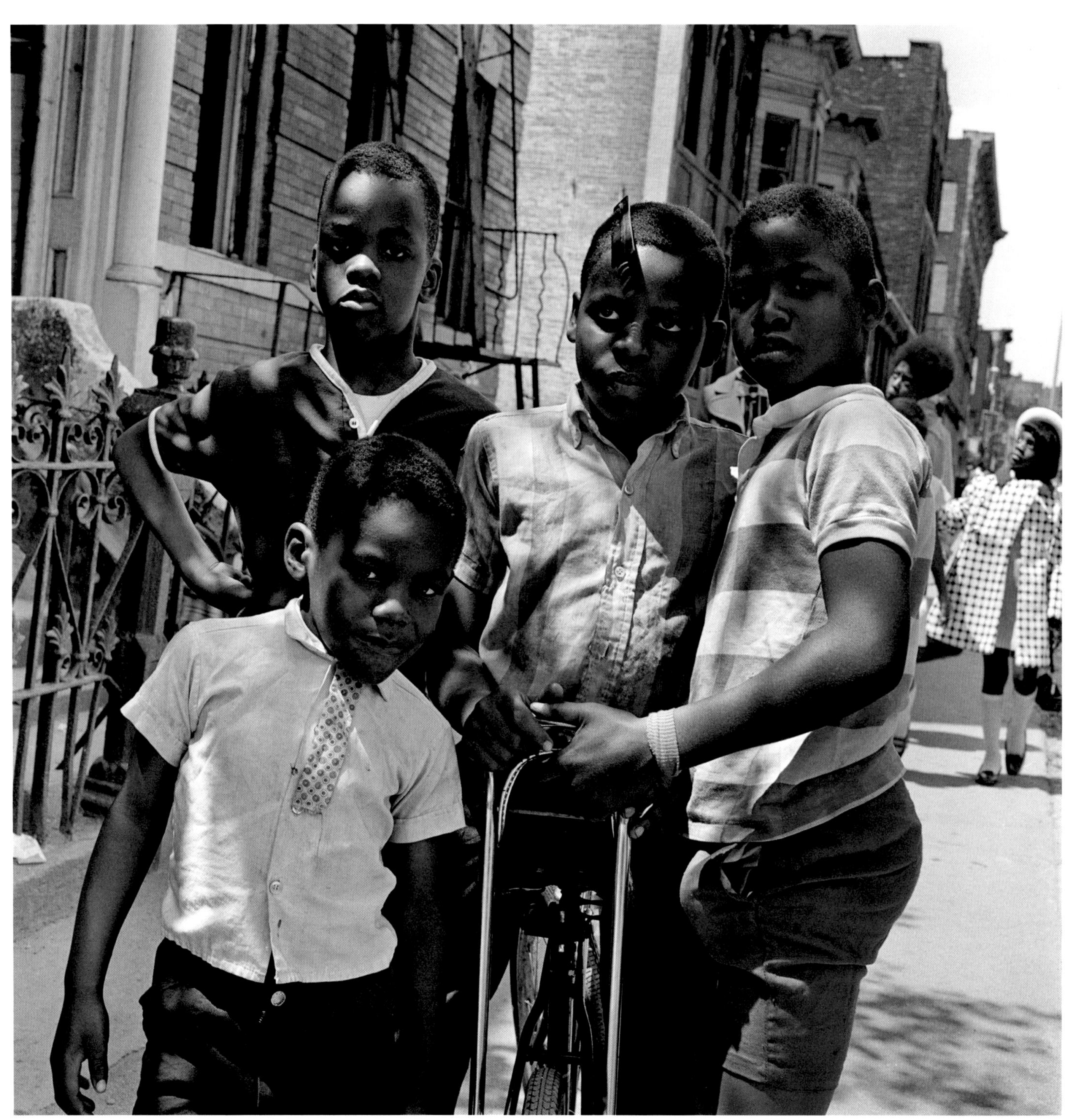

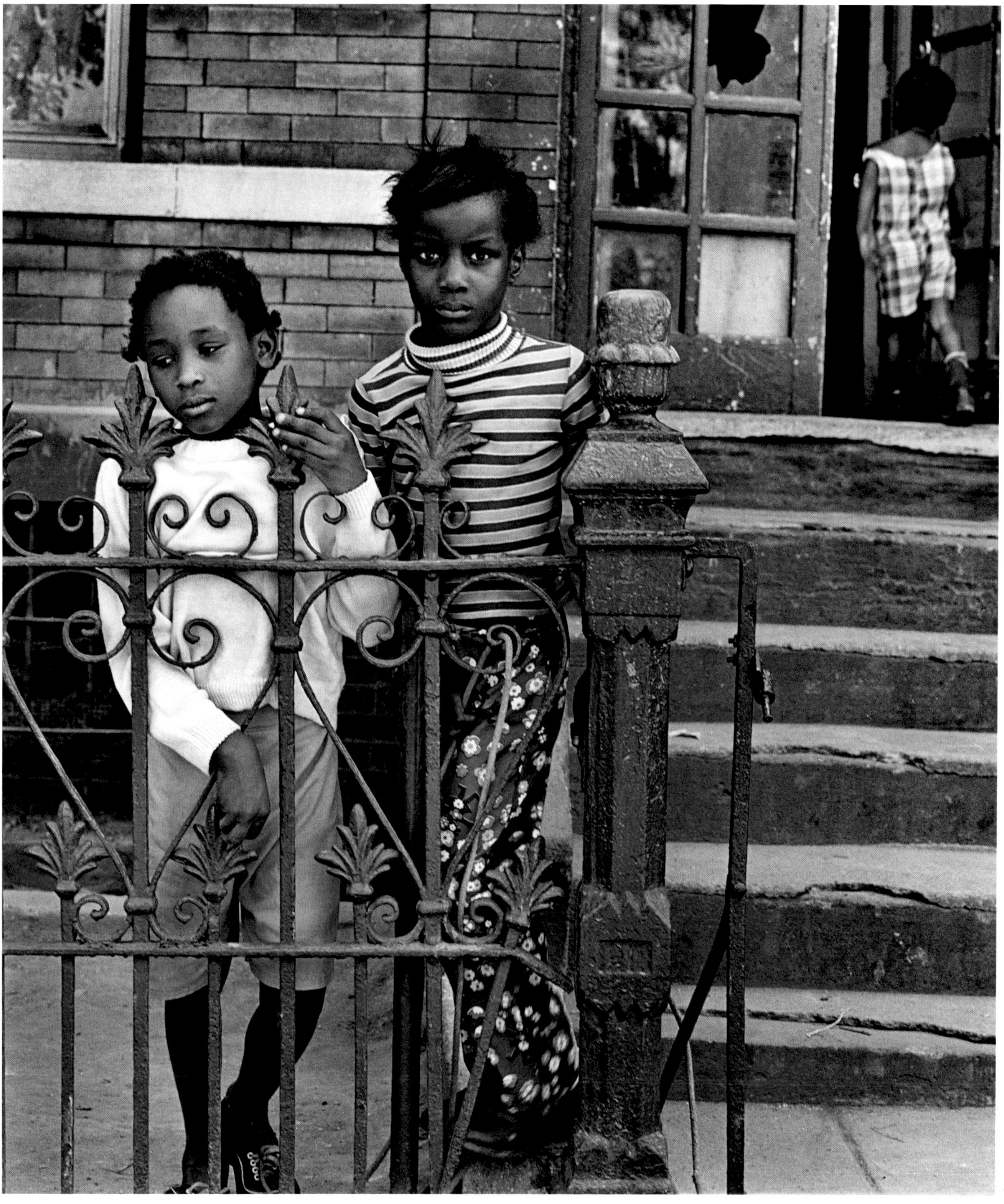

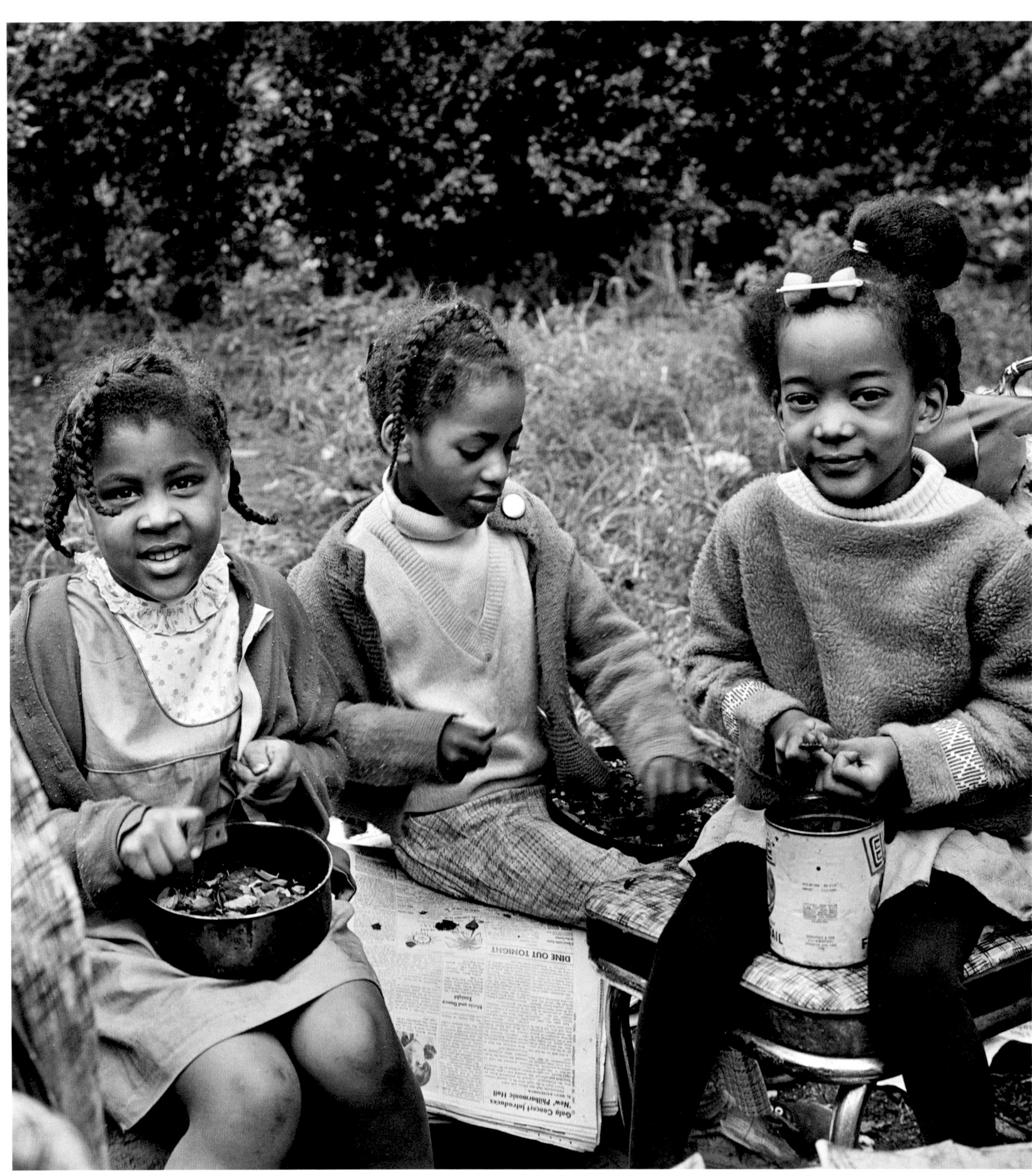

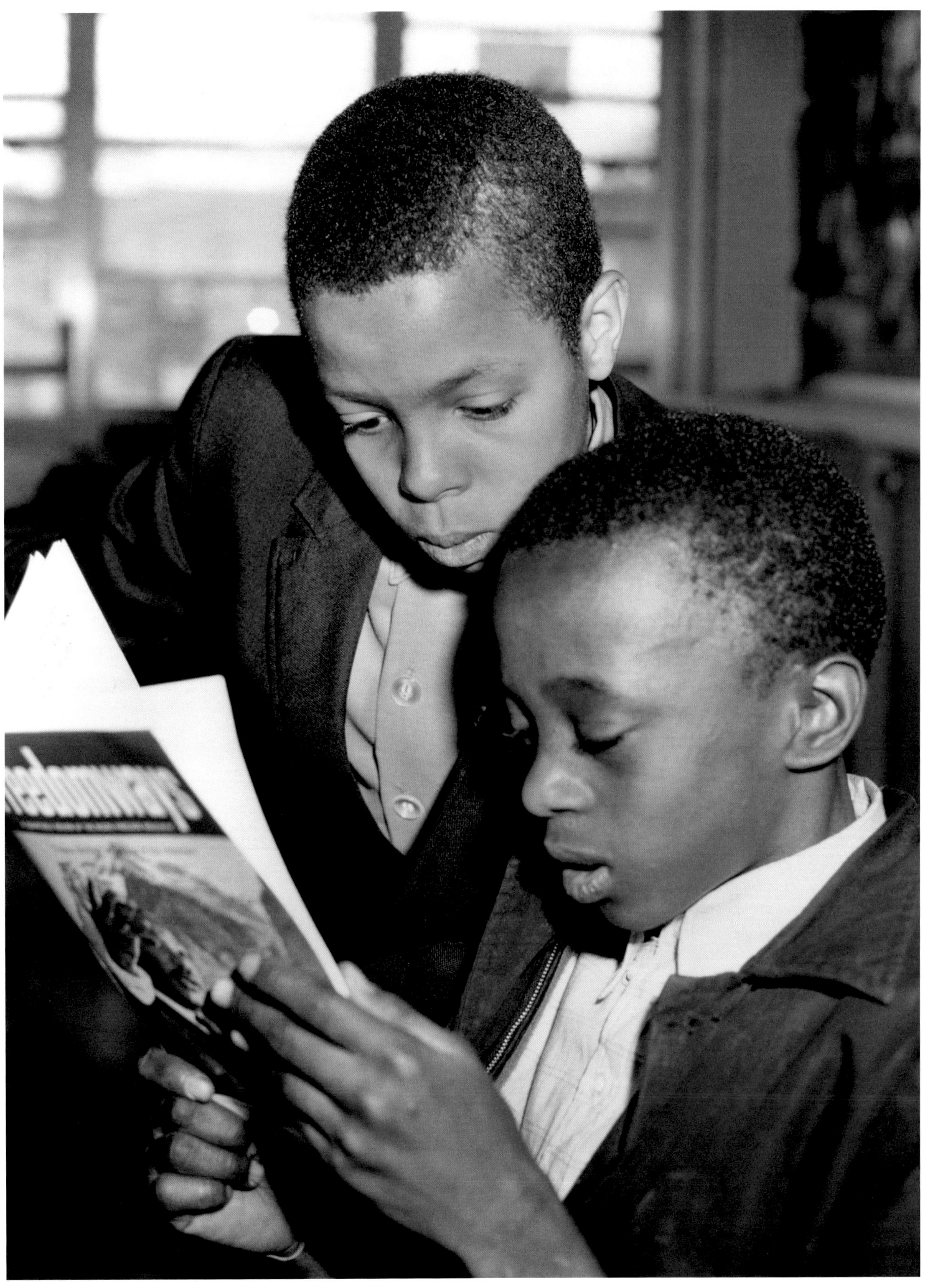

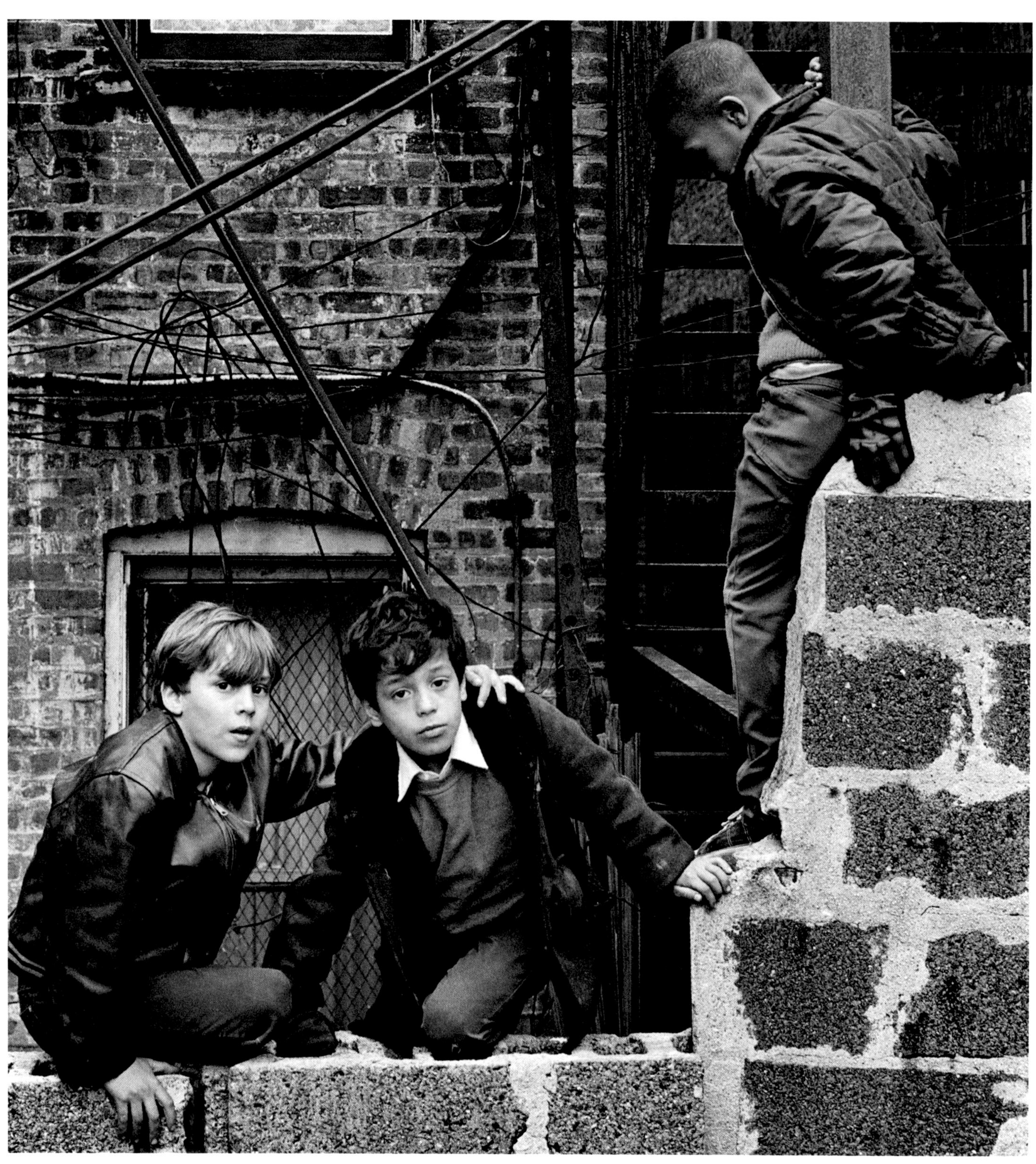

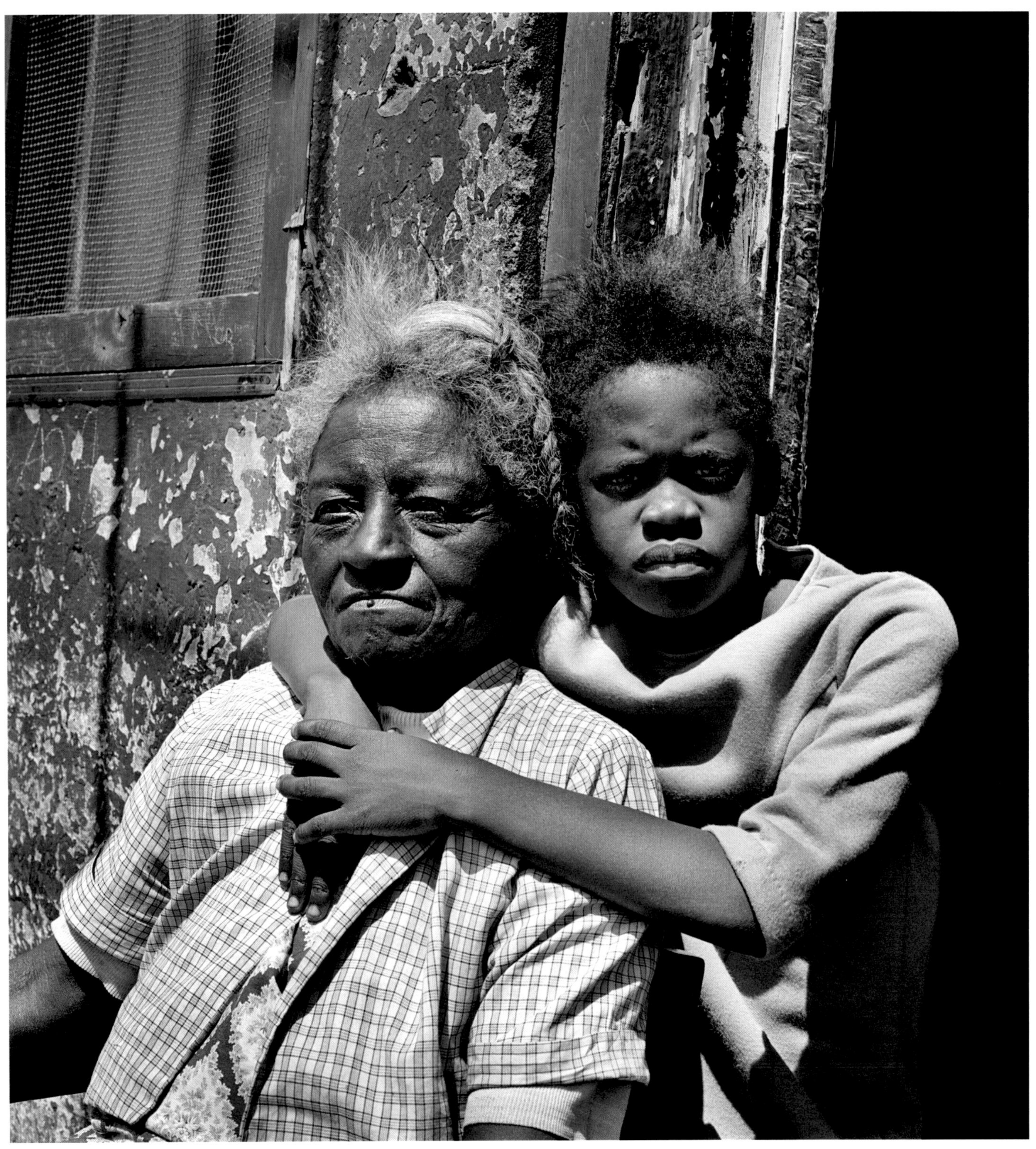

BUSHWICK

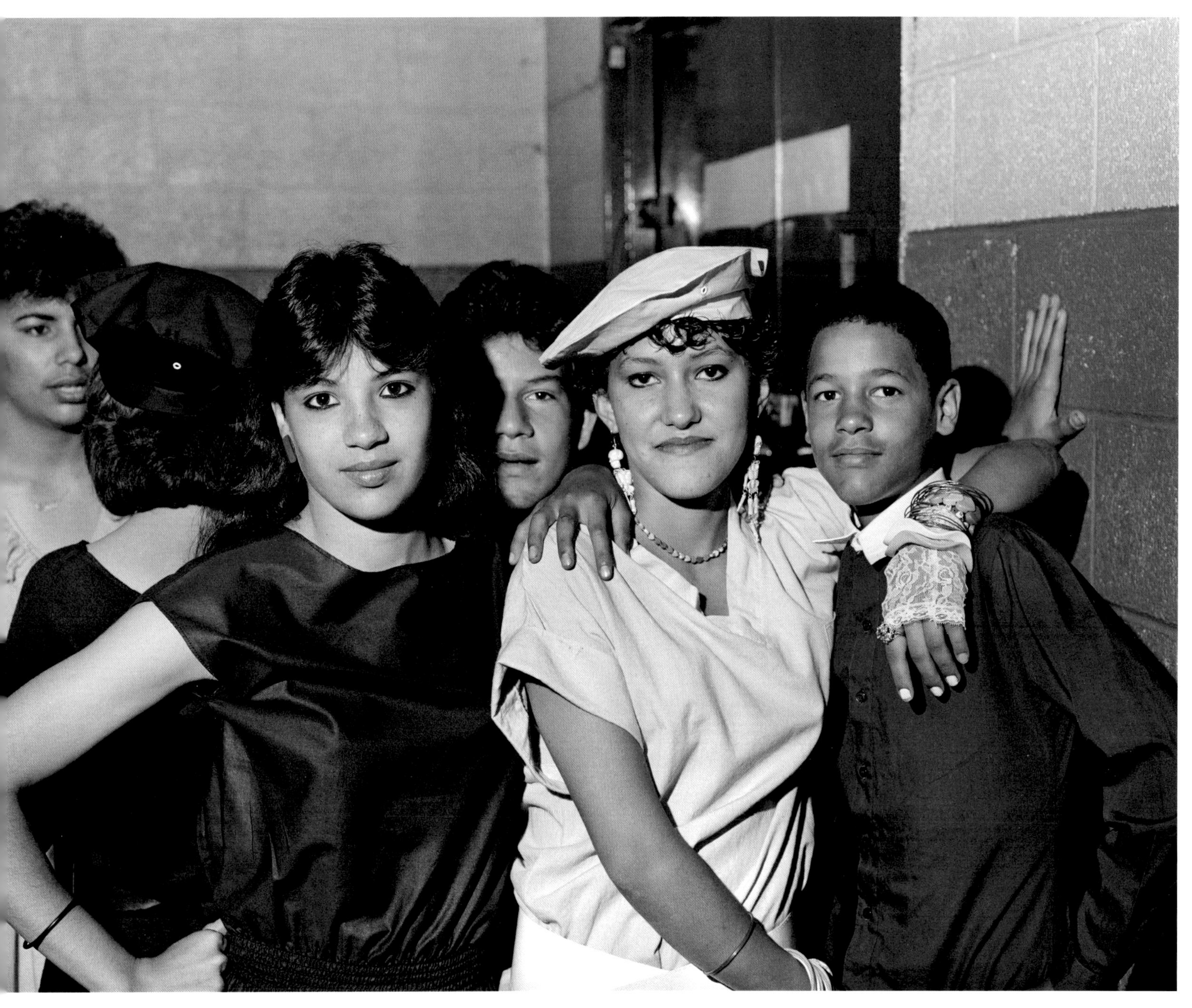

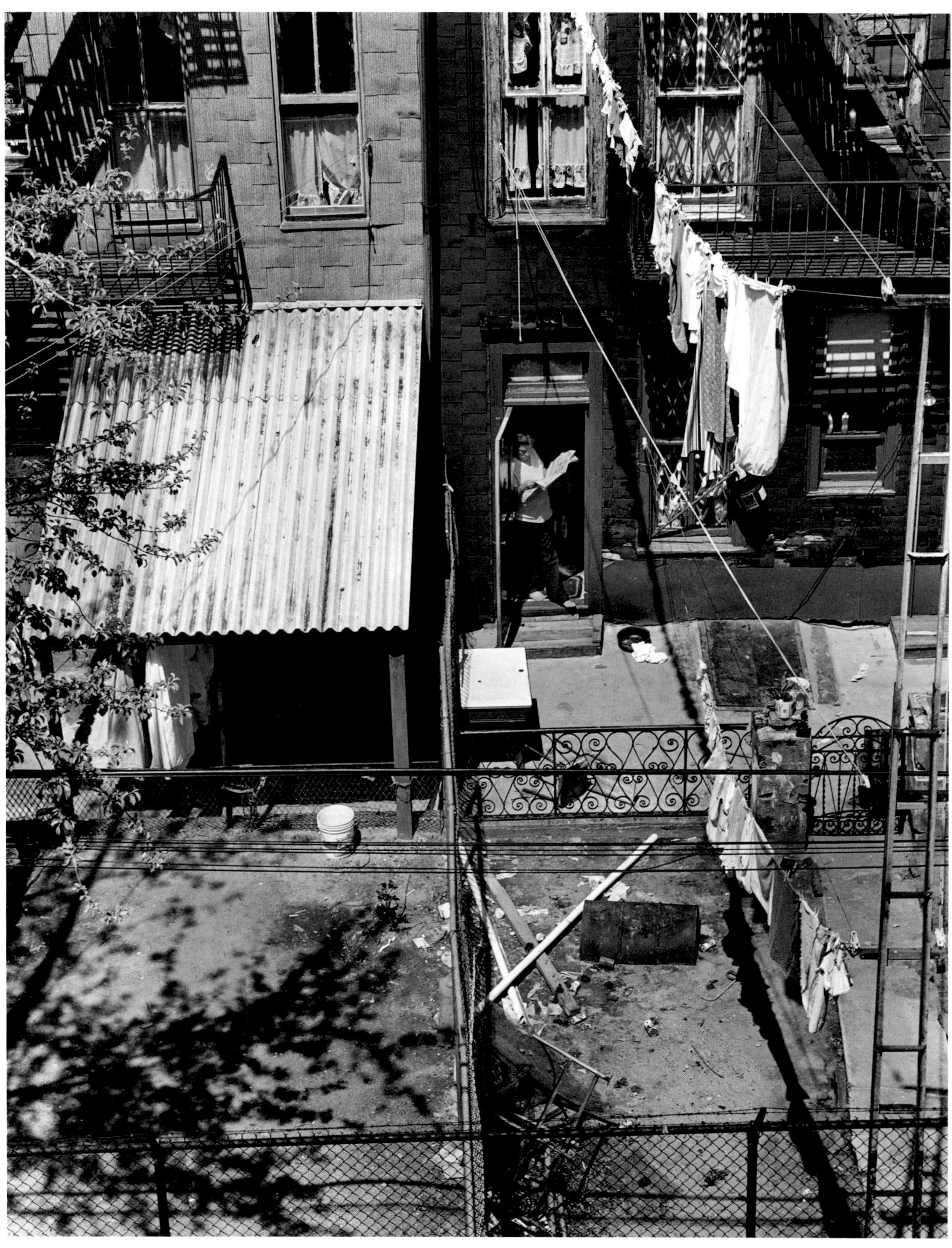

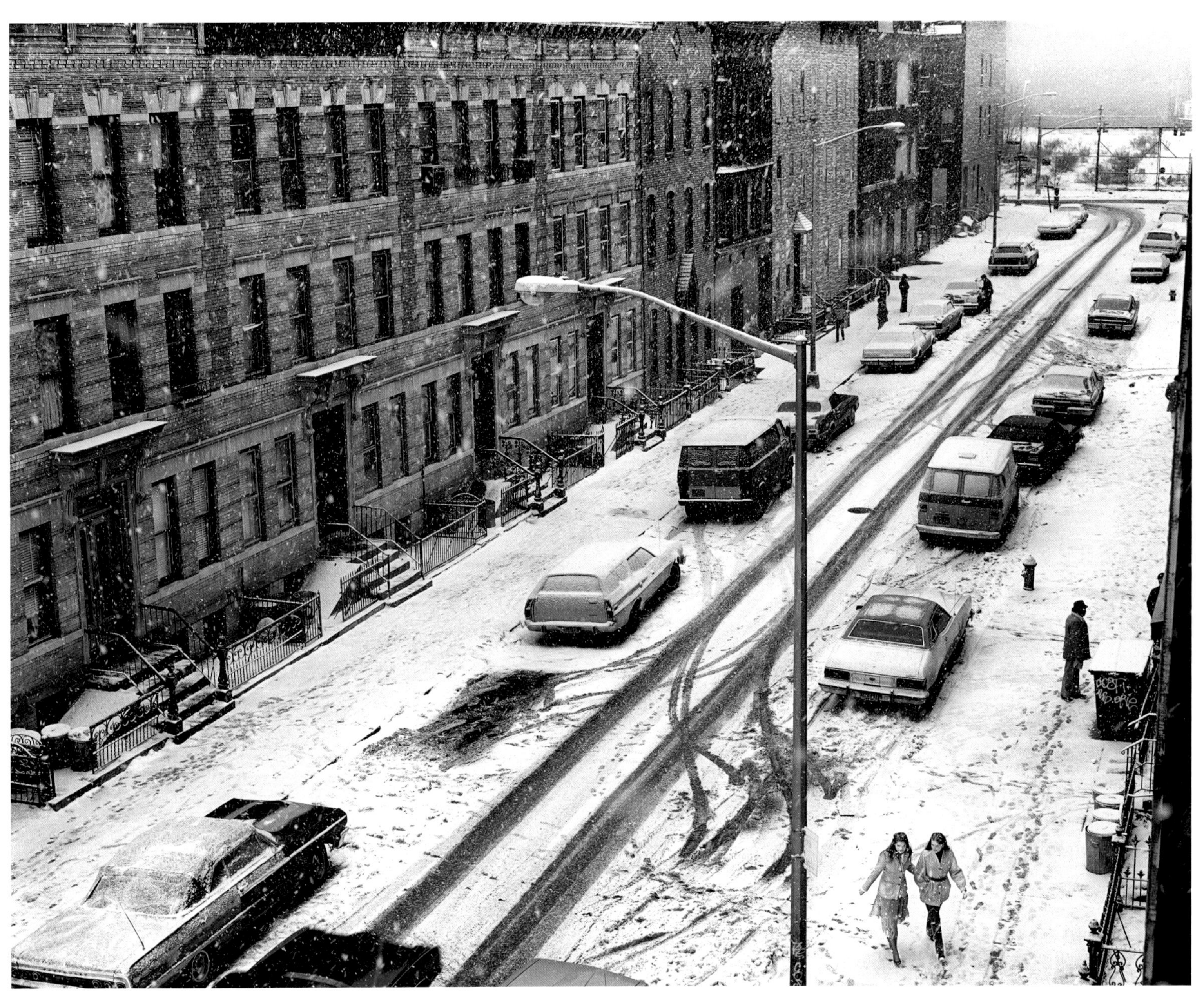

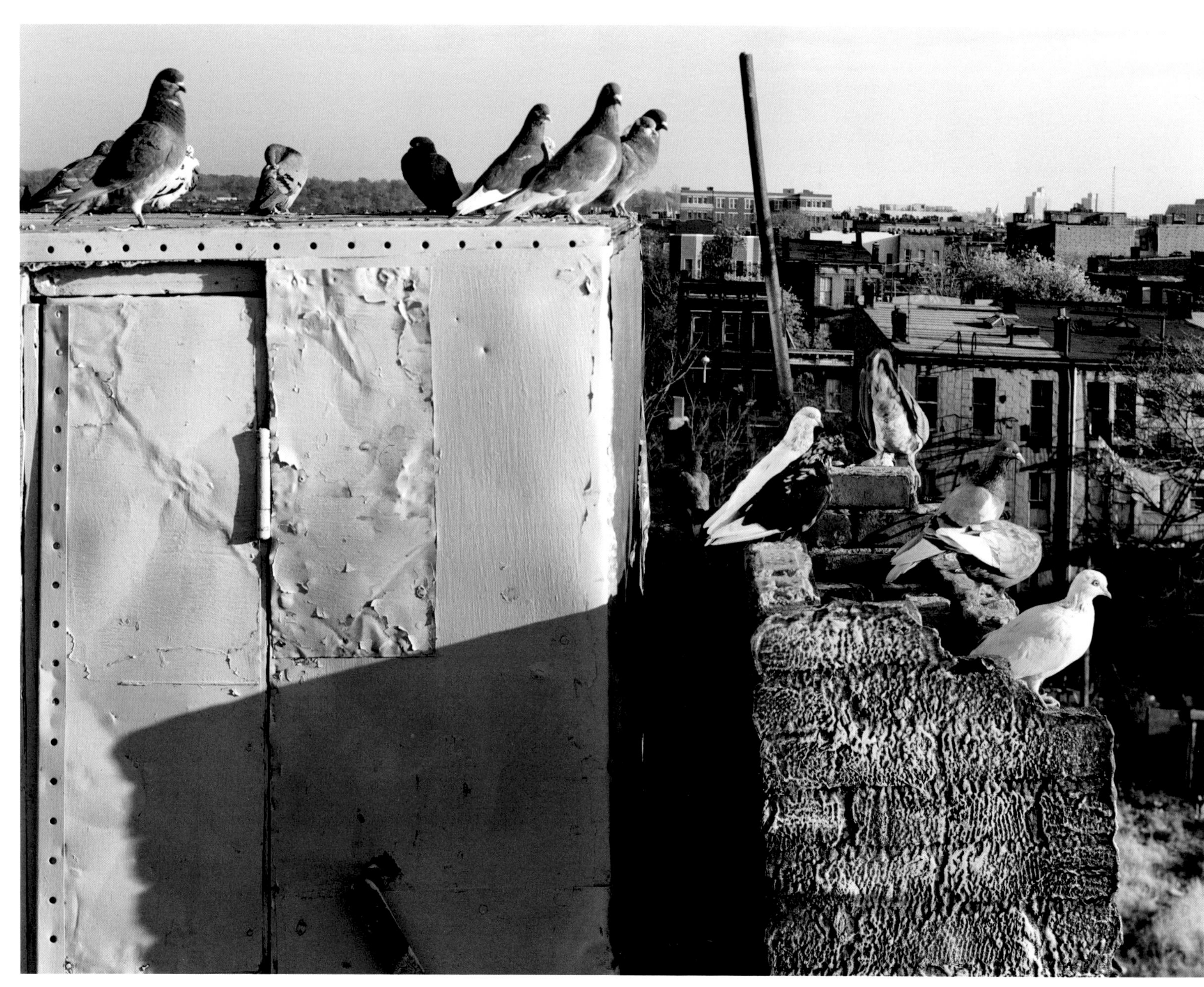

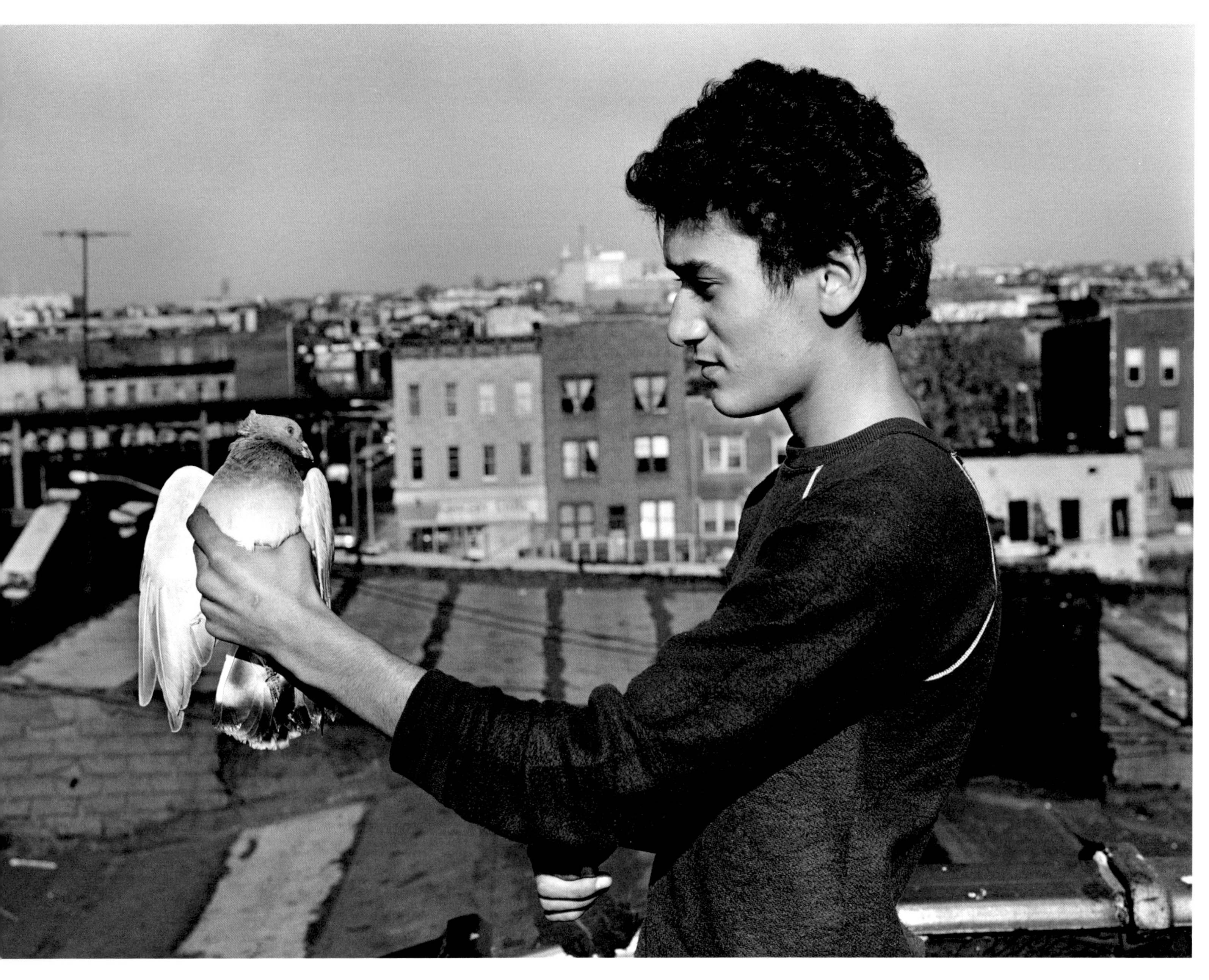

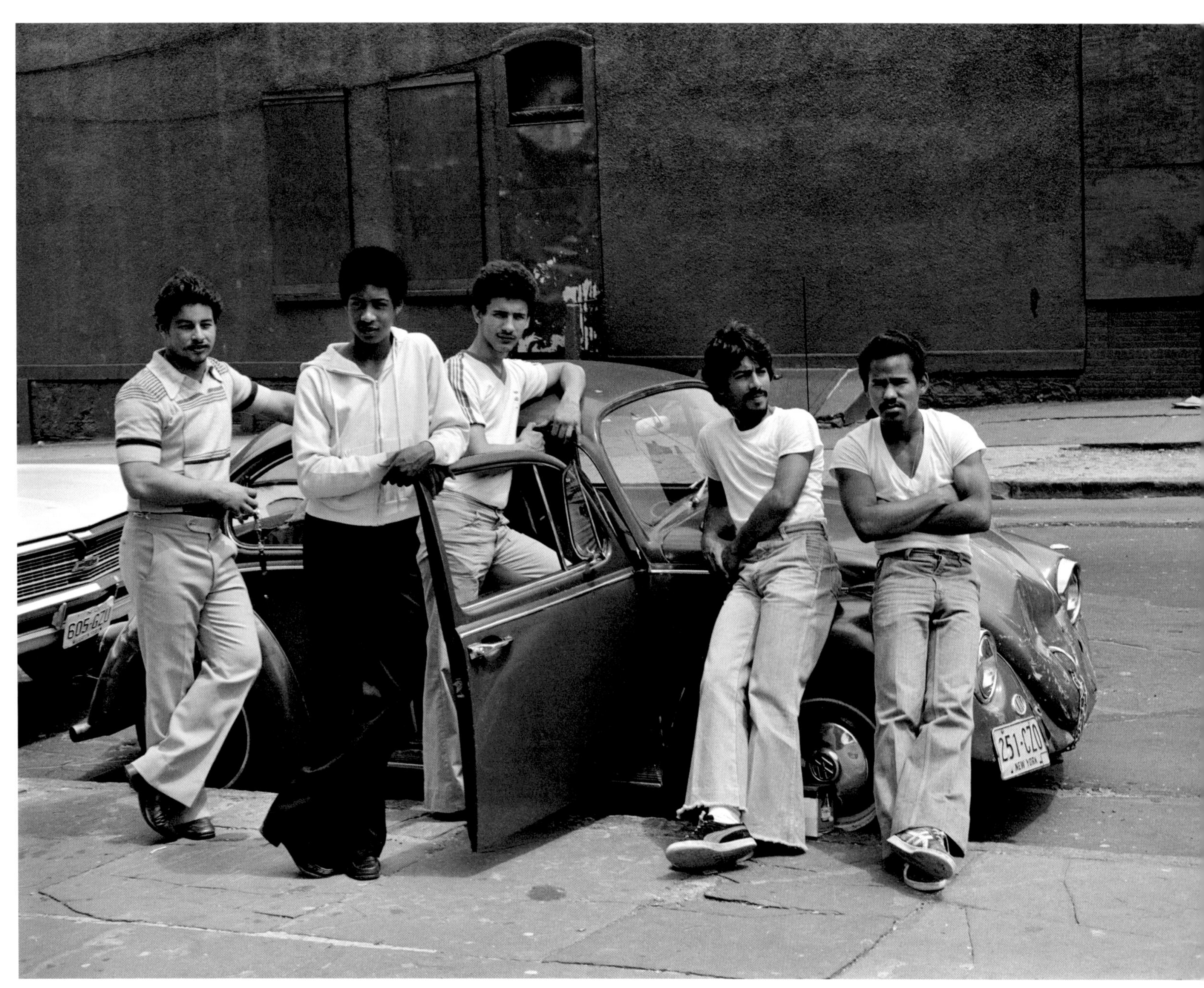

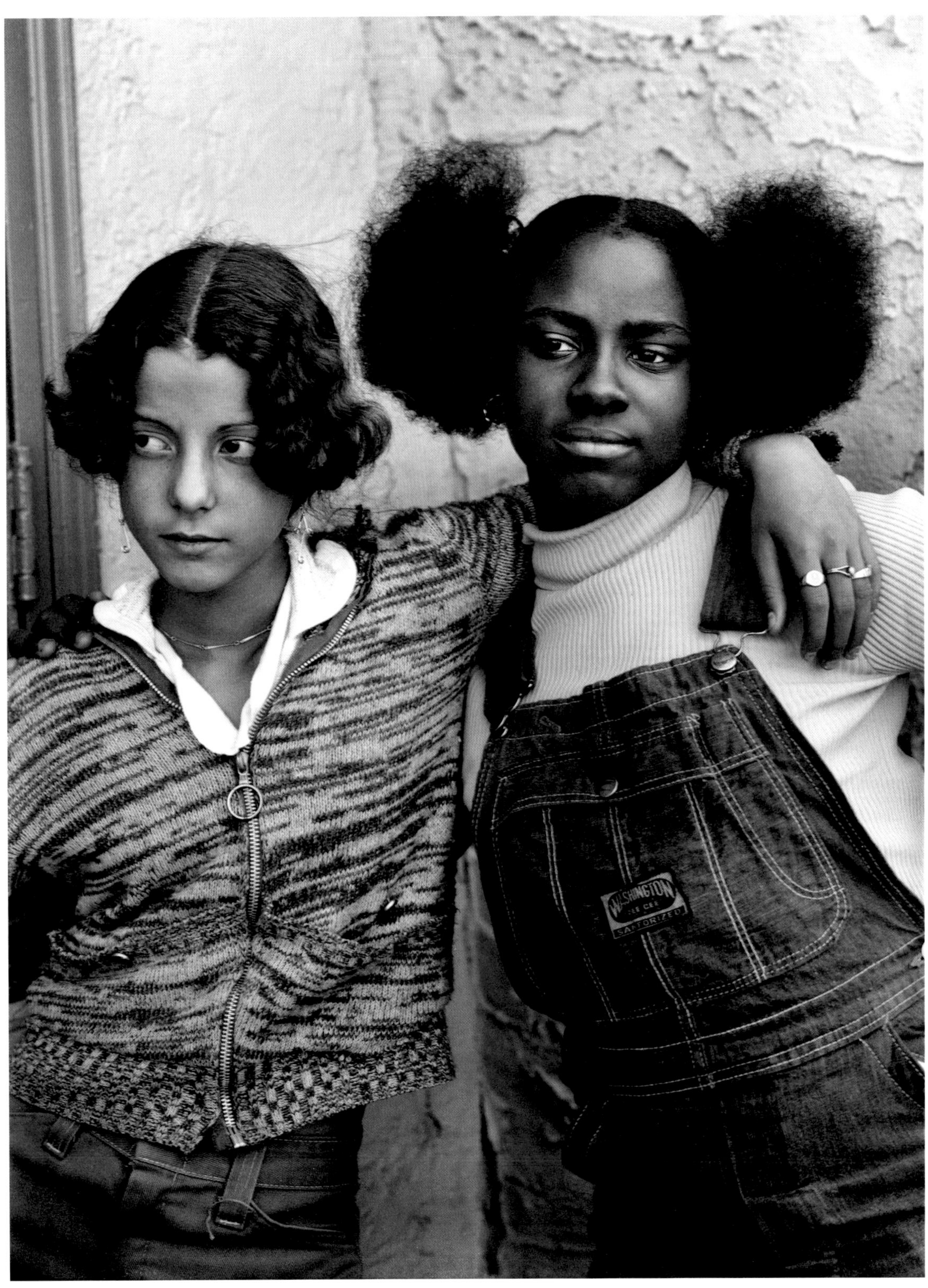

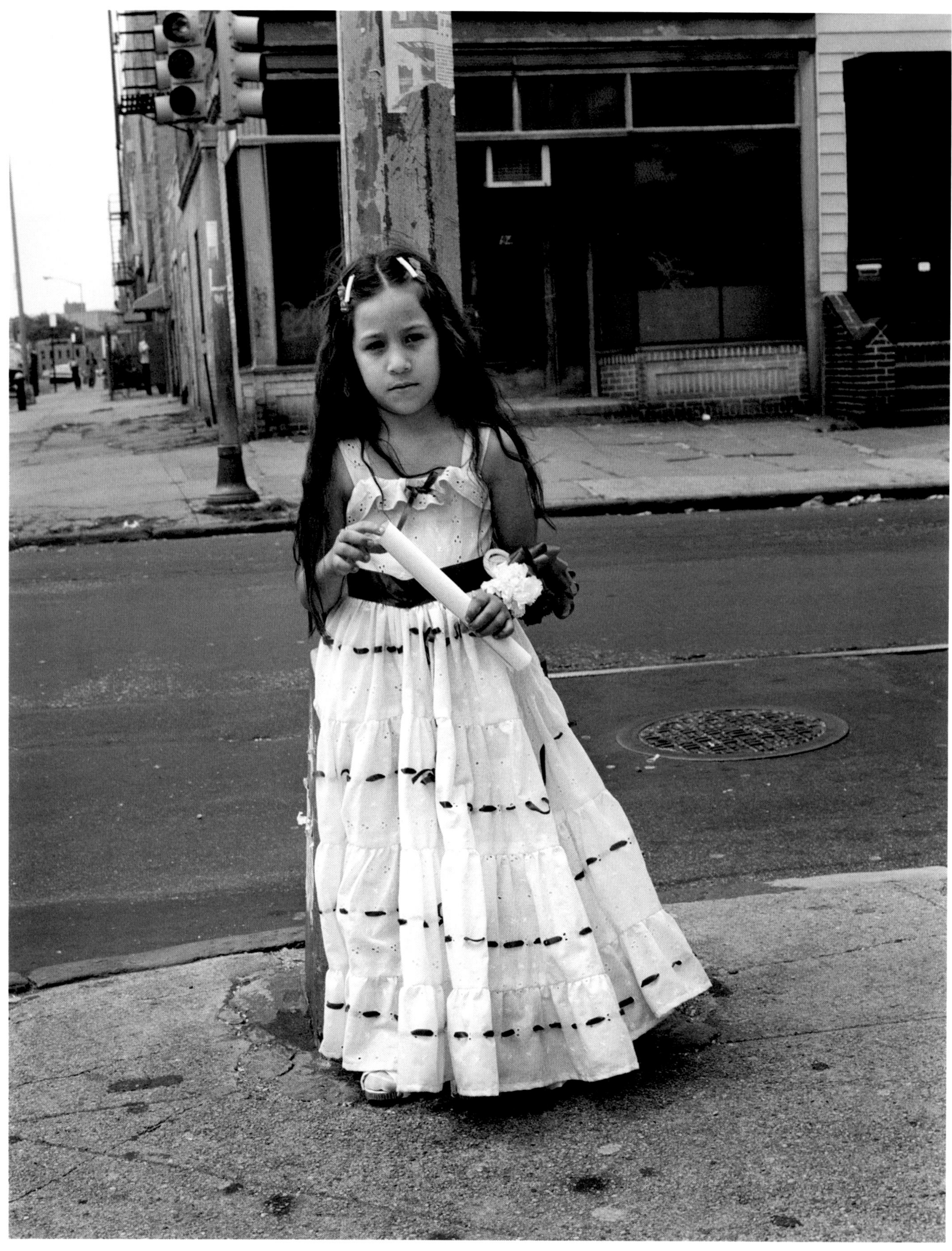

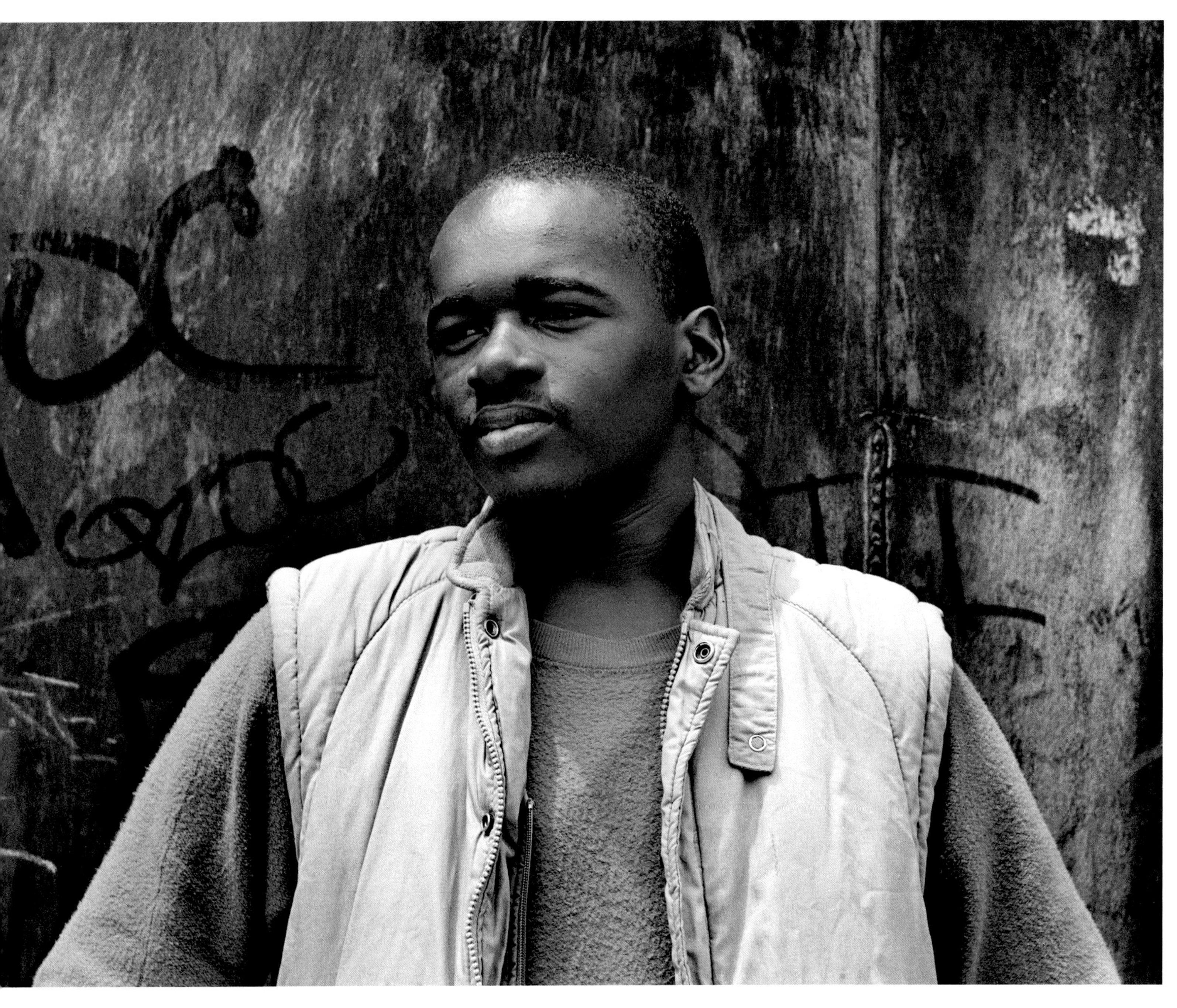

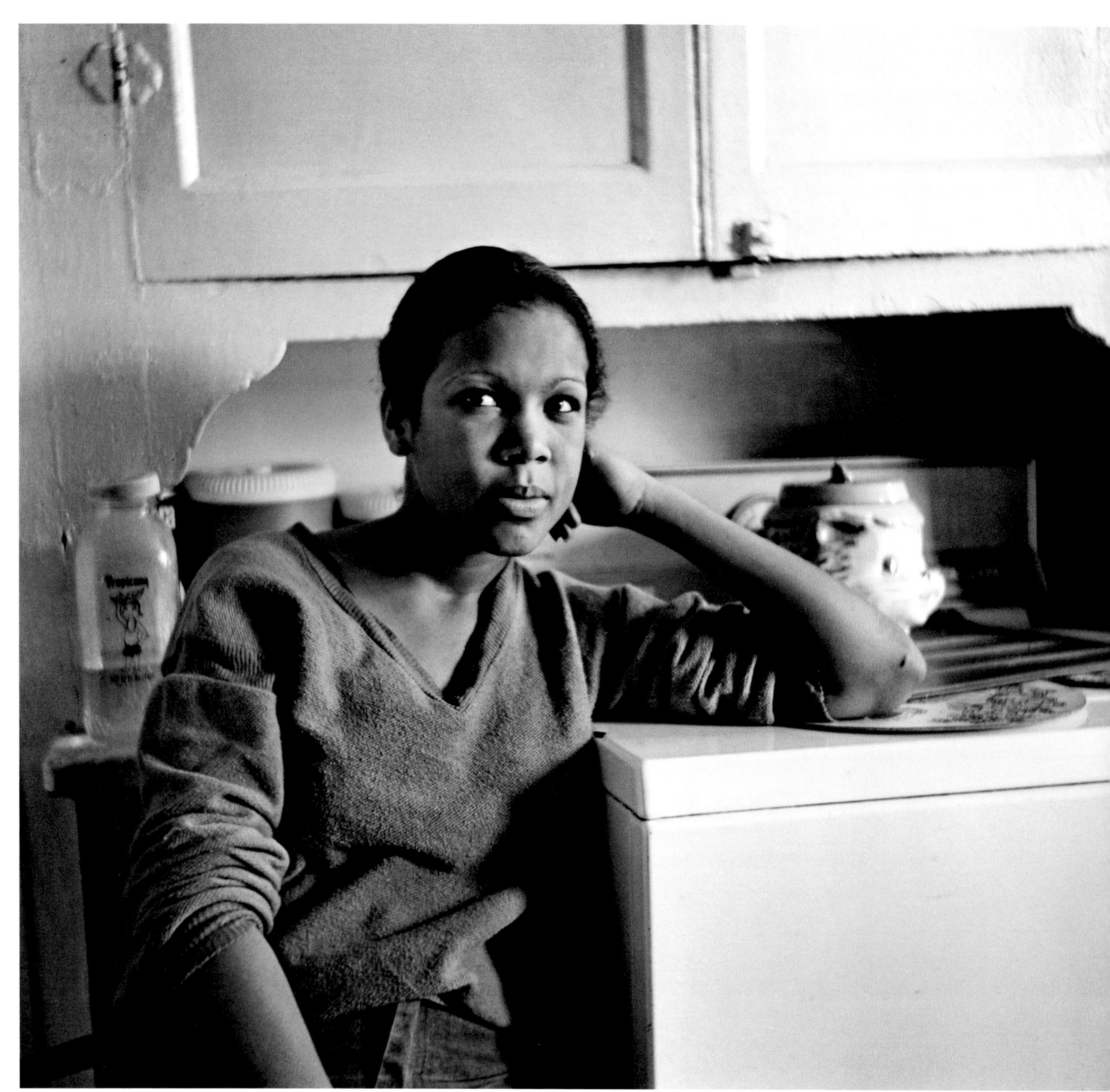

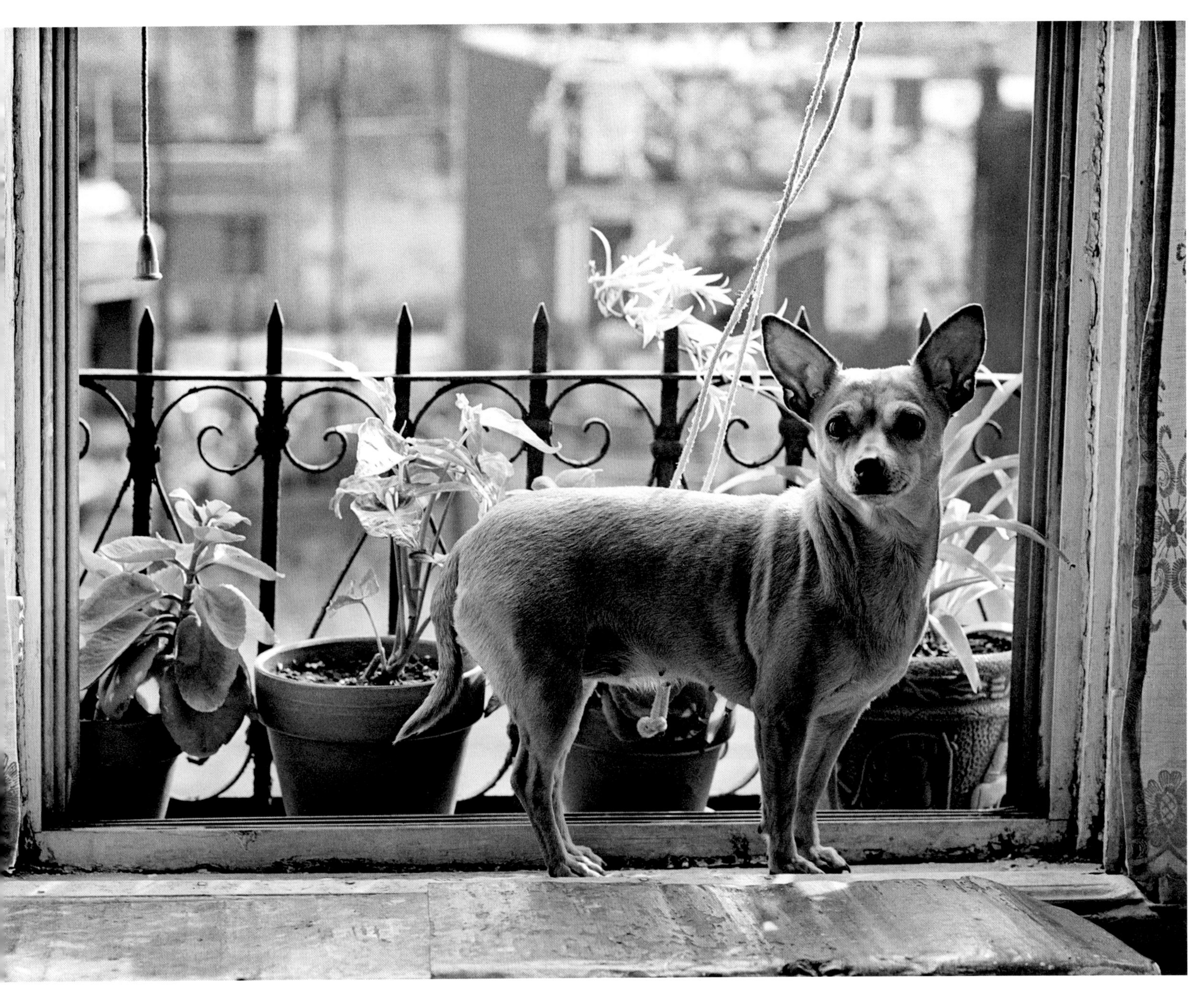

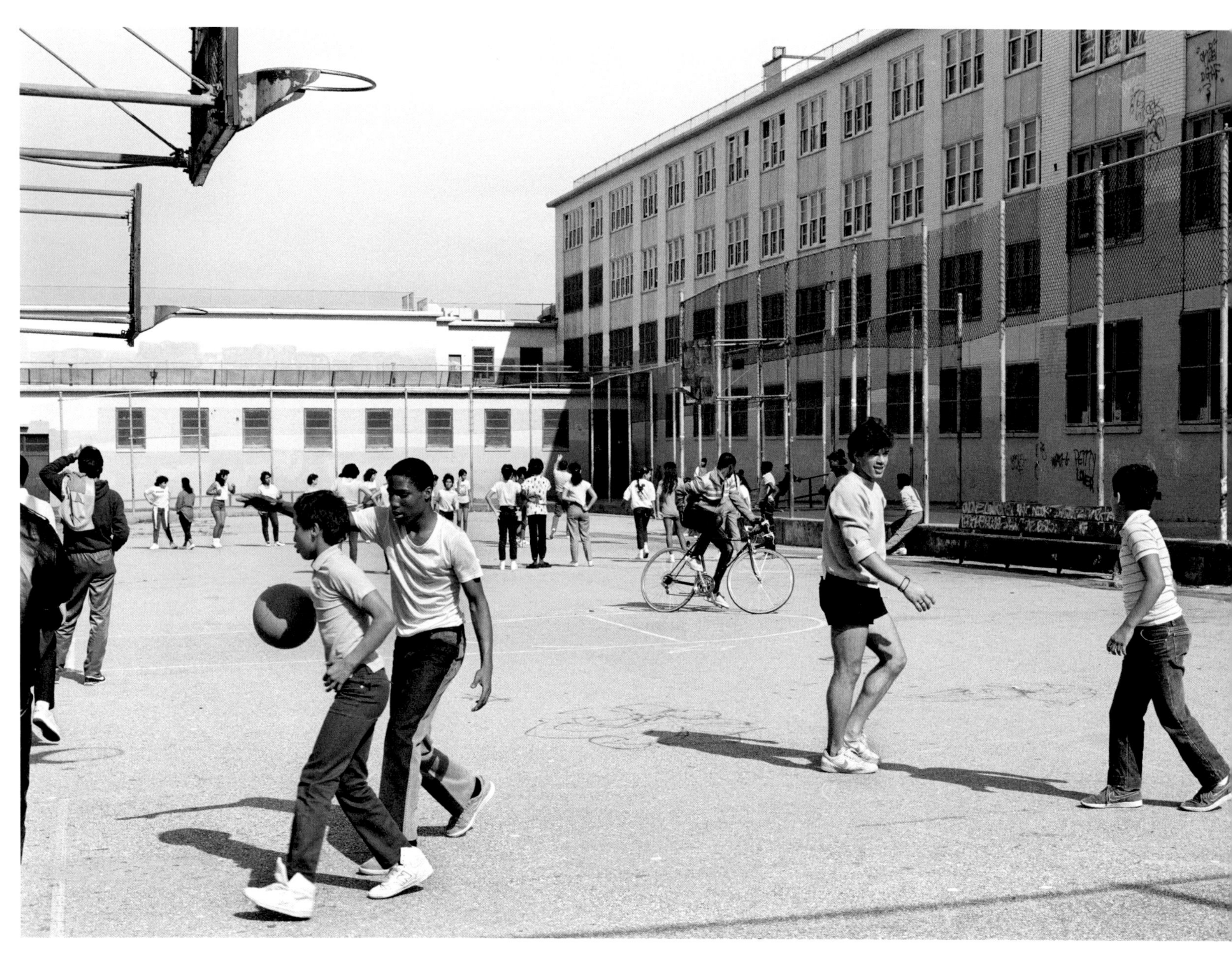

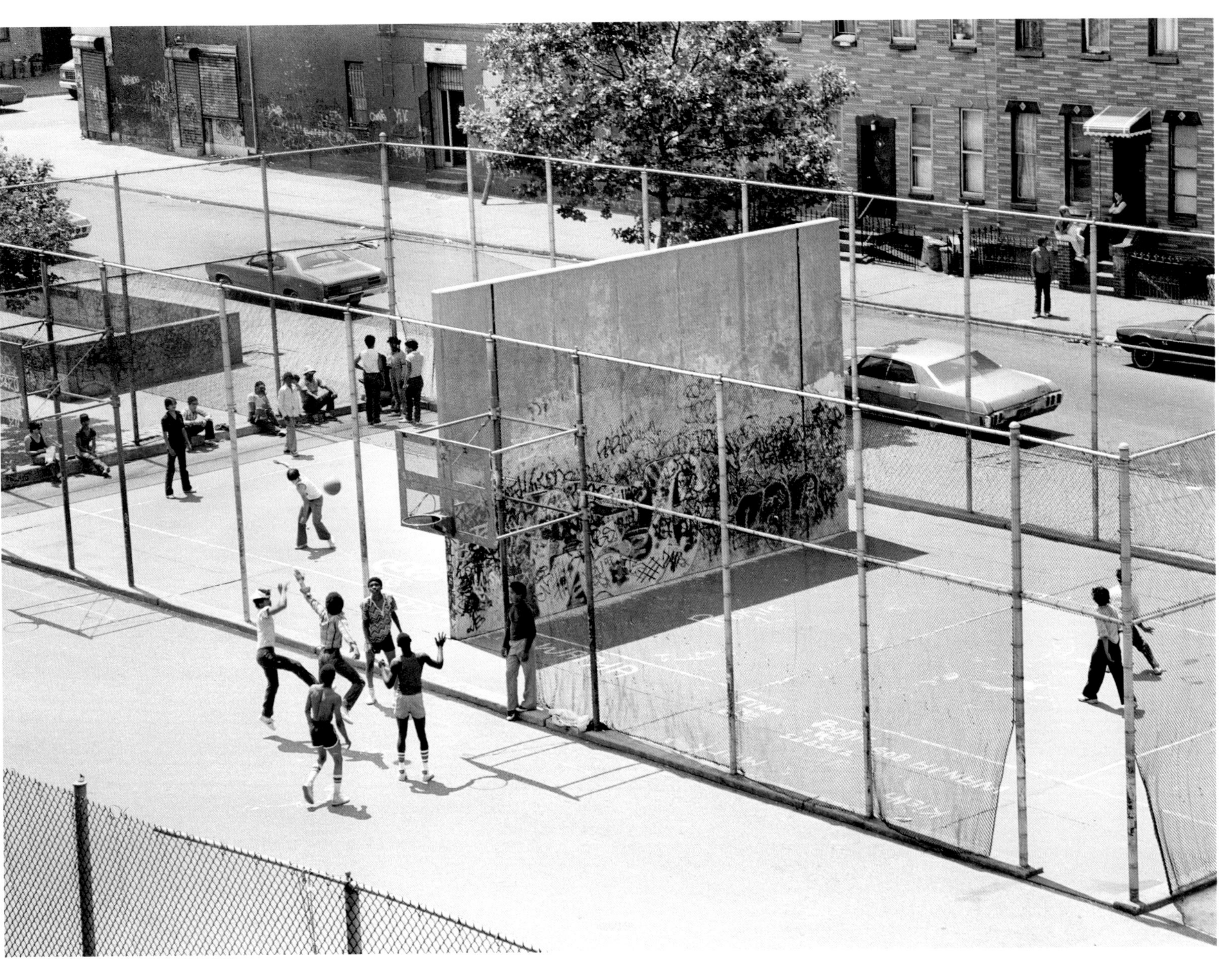

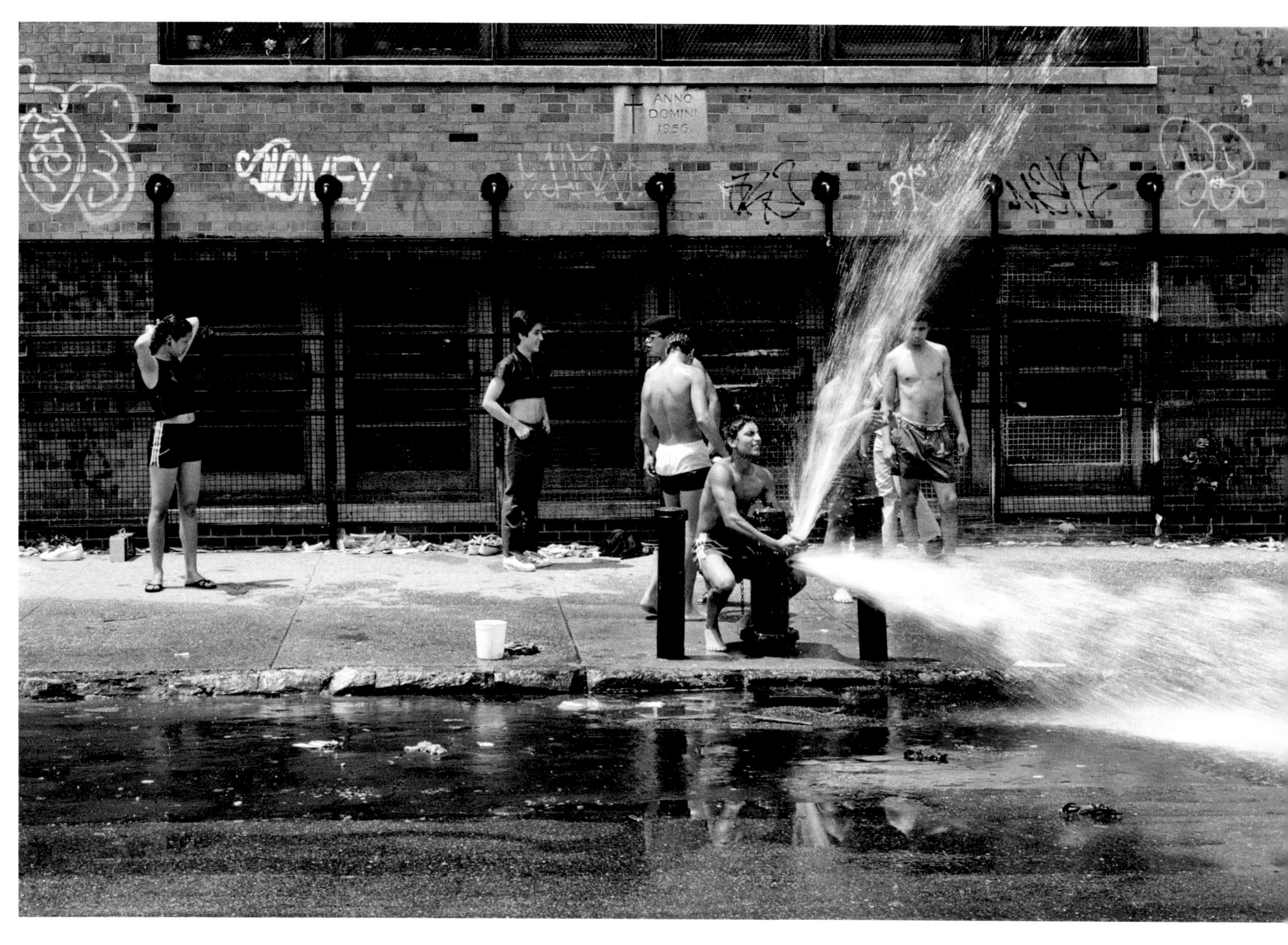

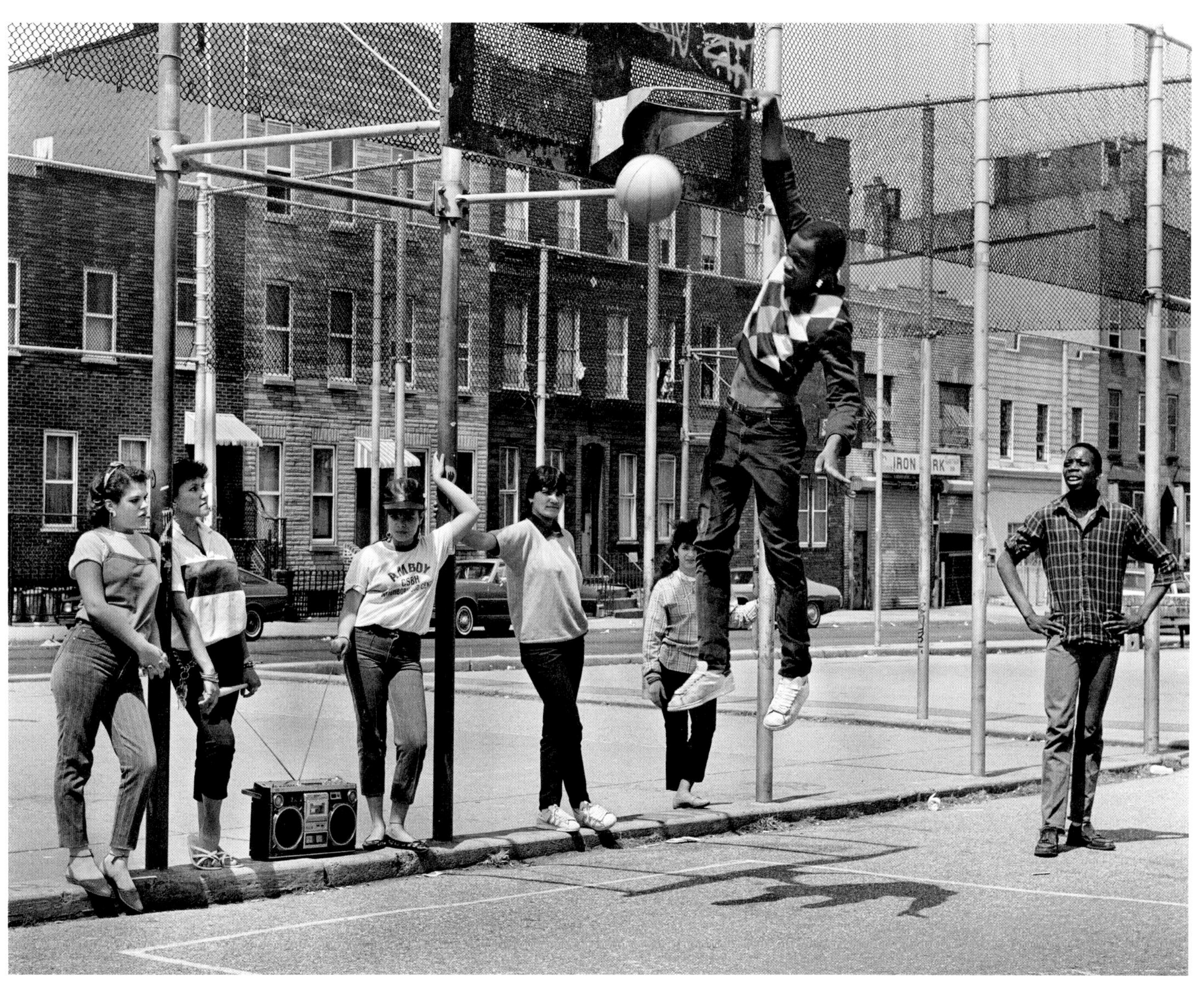

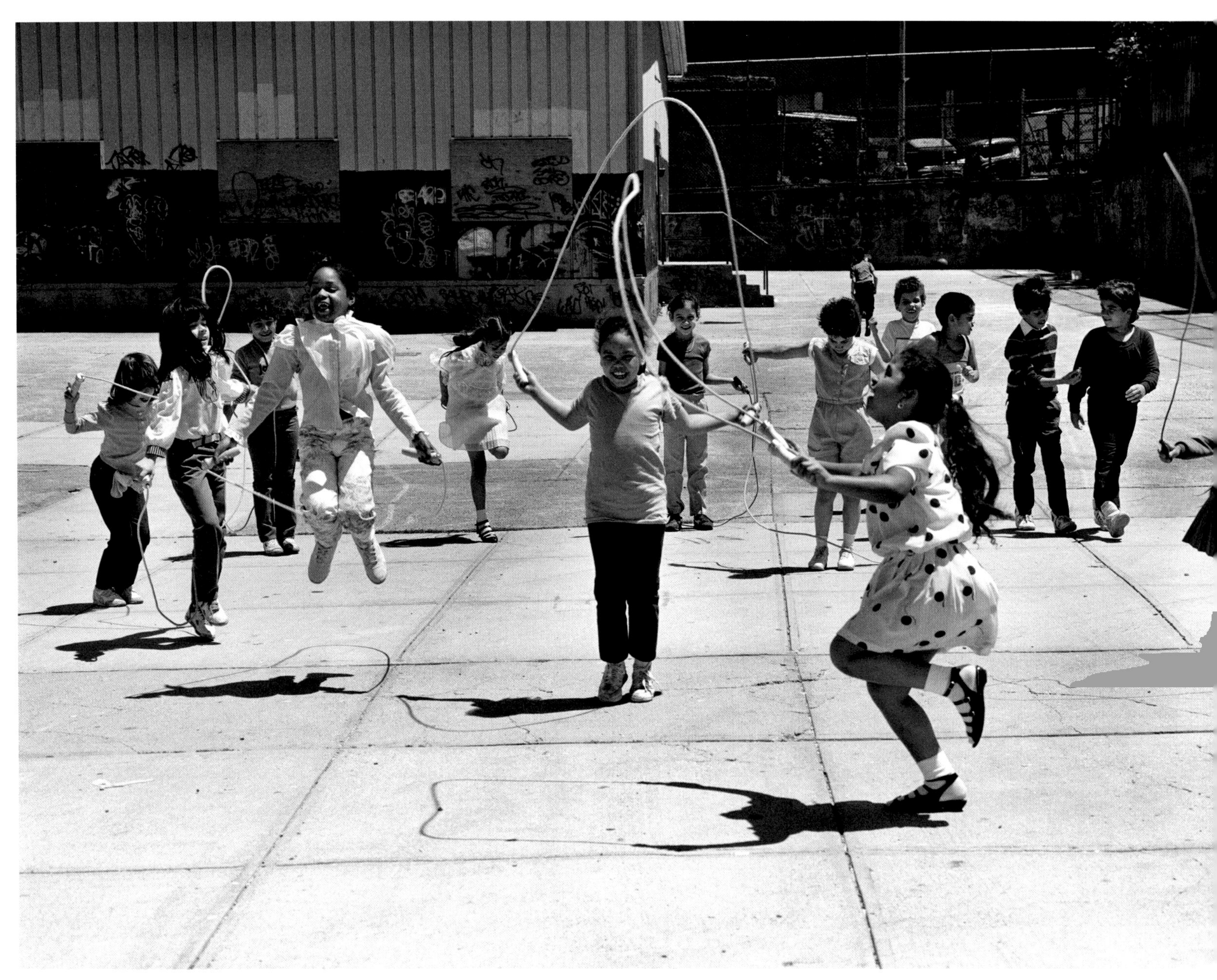

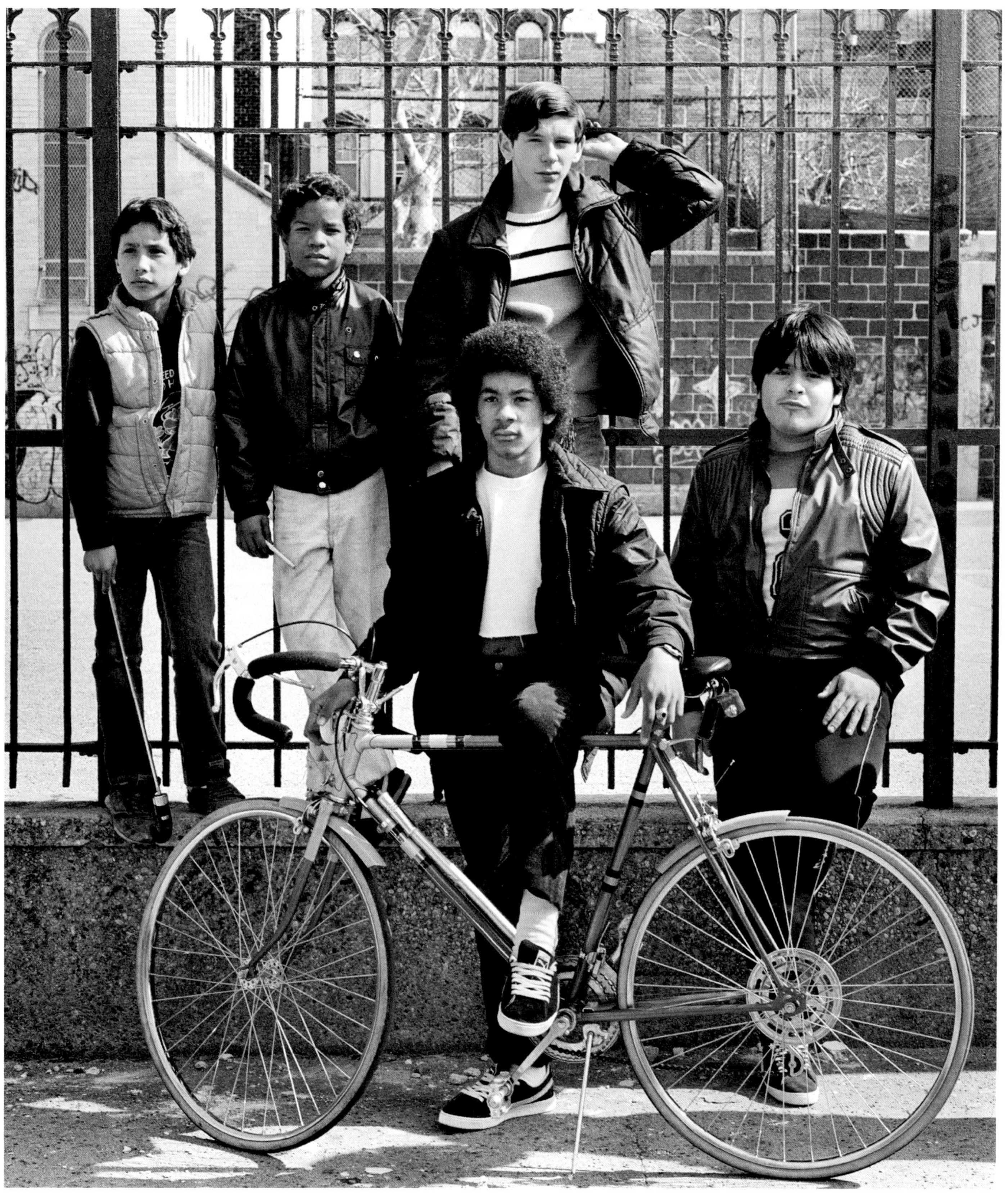

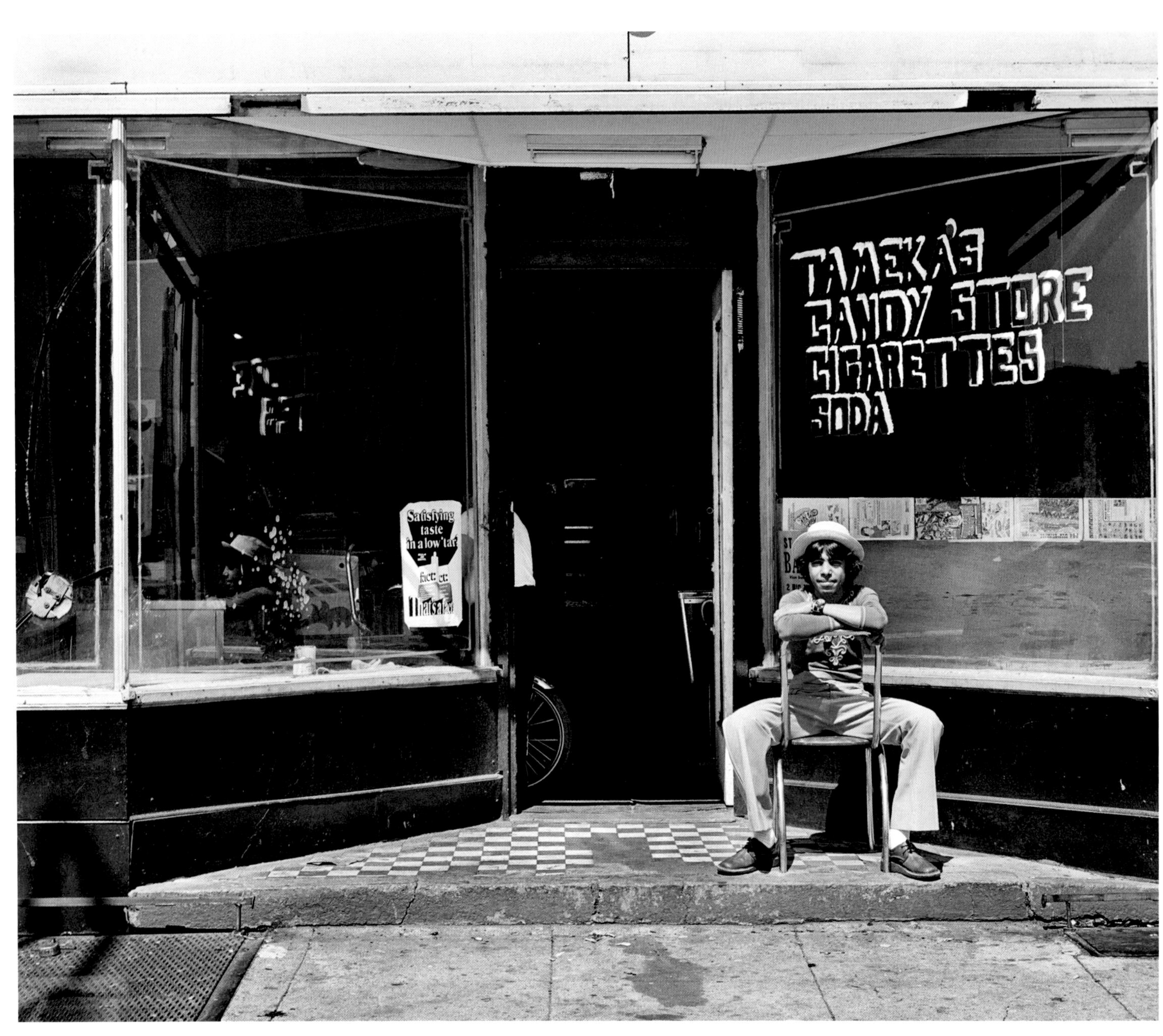

TAMEKA'S
CANDY STORE
CIGARETTES
SODA
Satisfying
taste
in a low 'tar

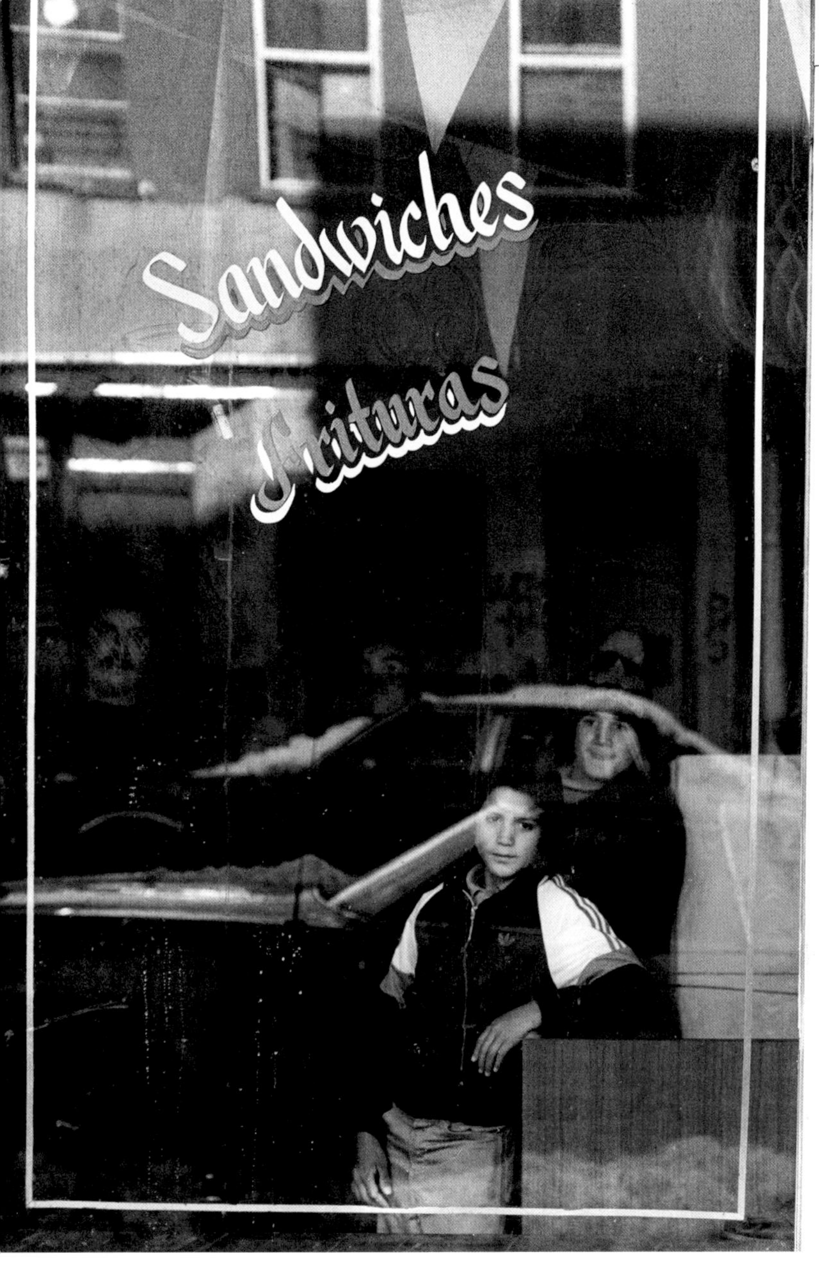
Sandwiches
Frituras
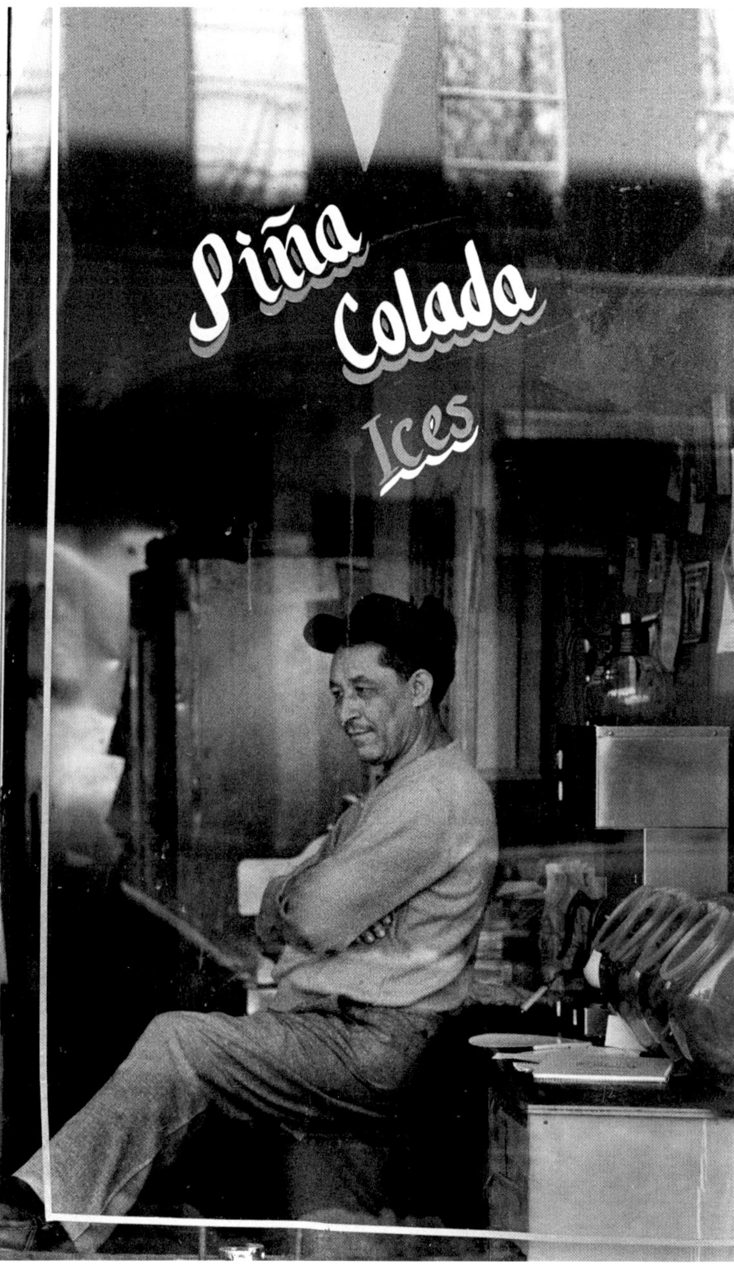
Piña
Colada
Ices

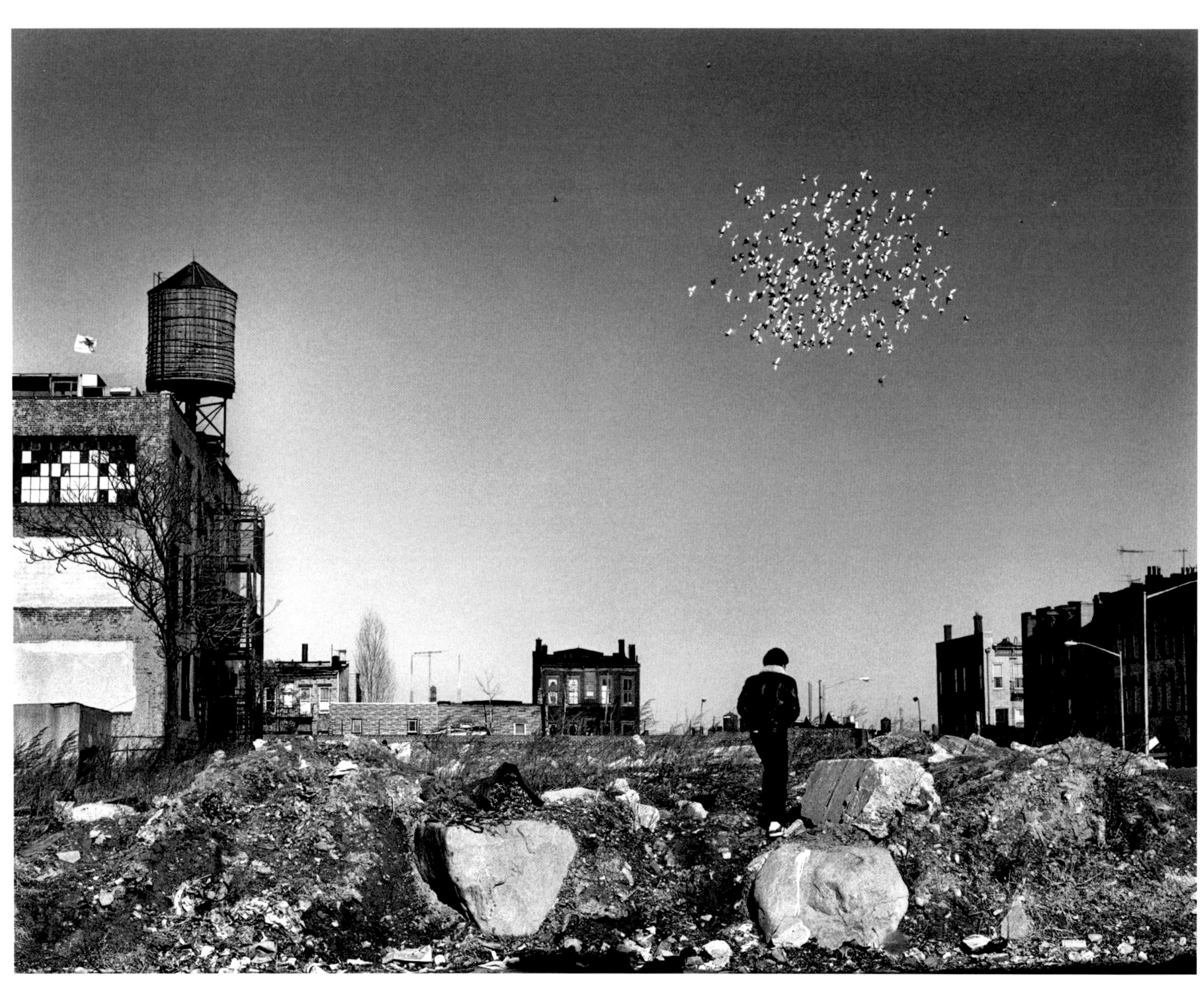

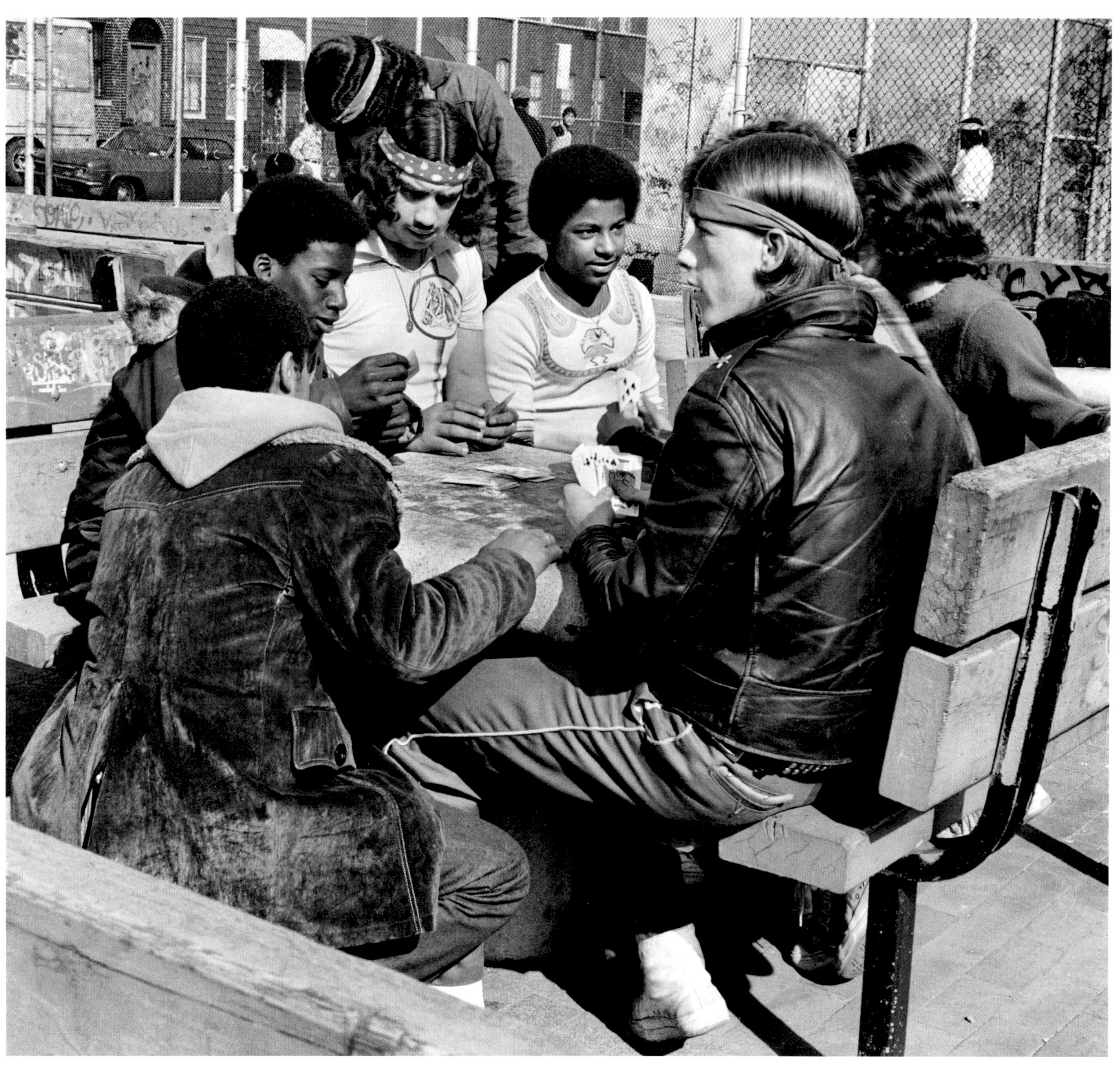

ALTERNATIVE HIGH SCHOOOL STUDENTS

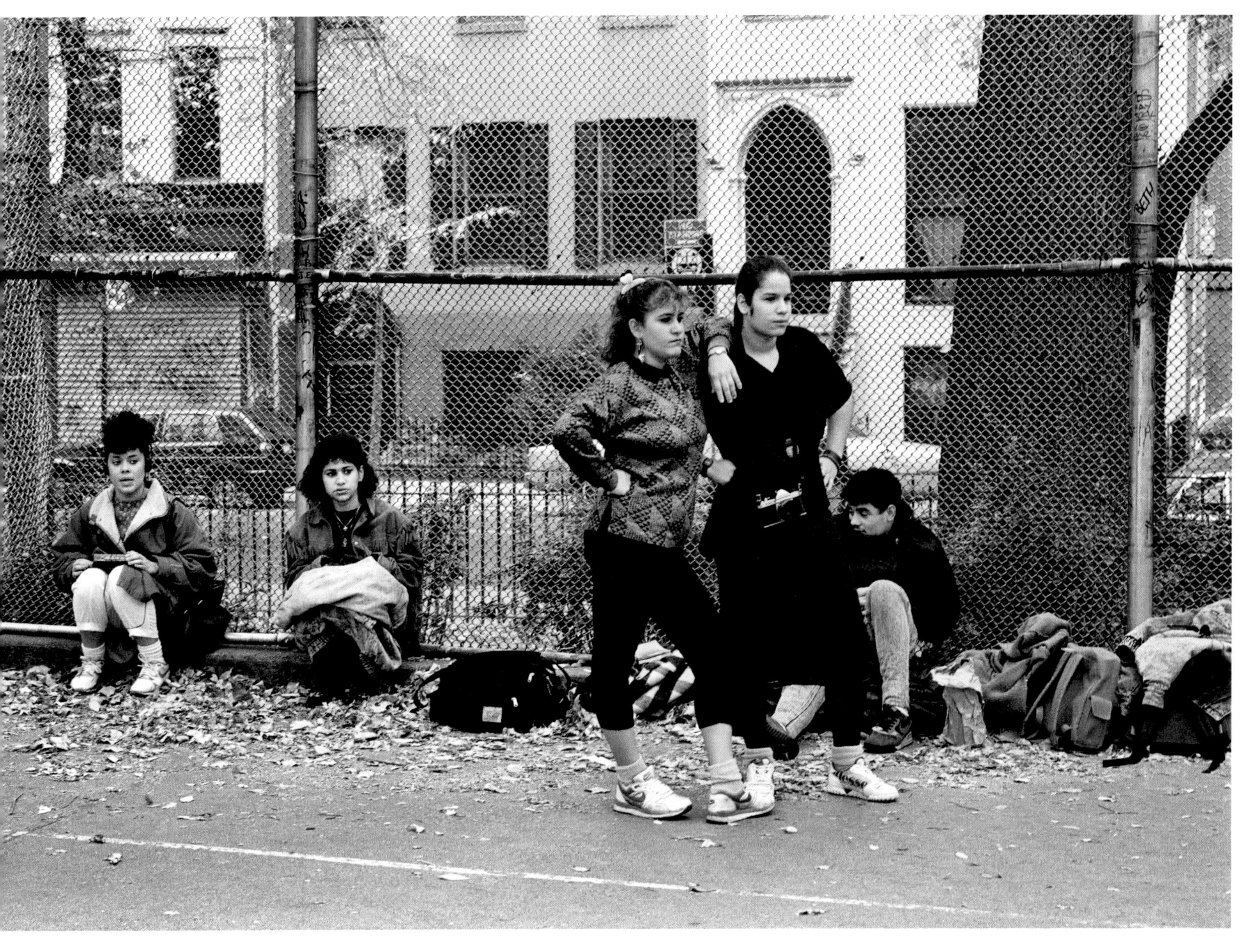

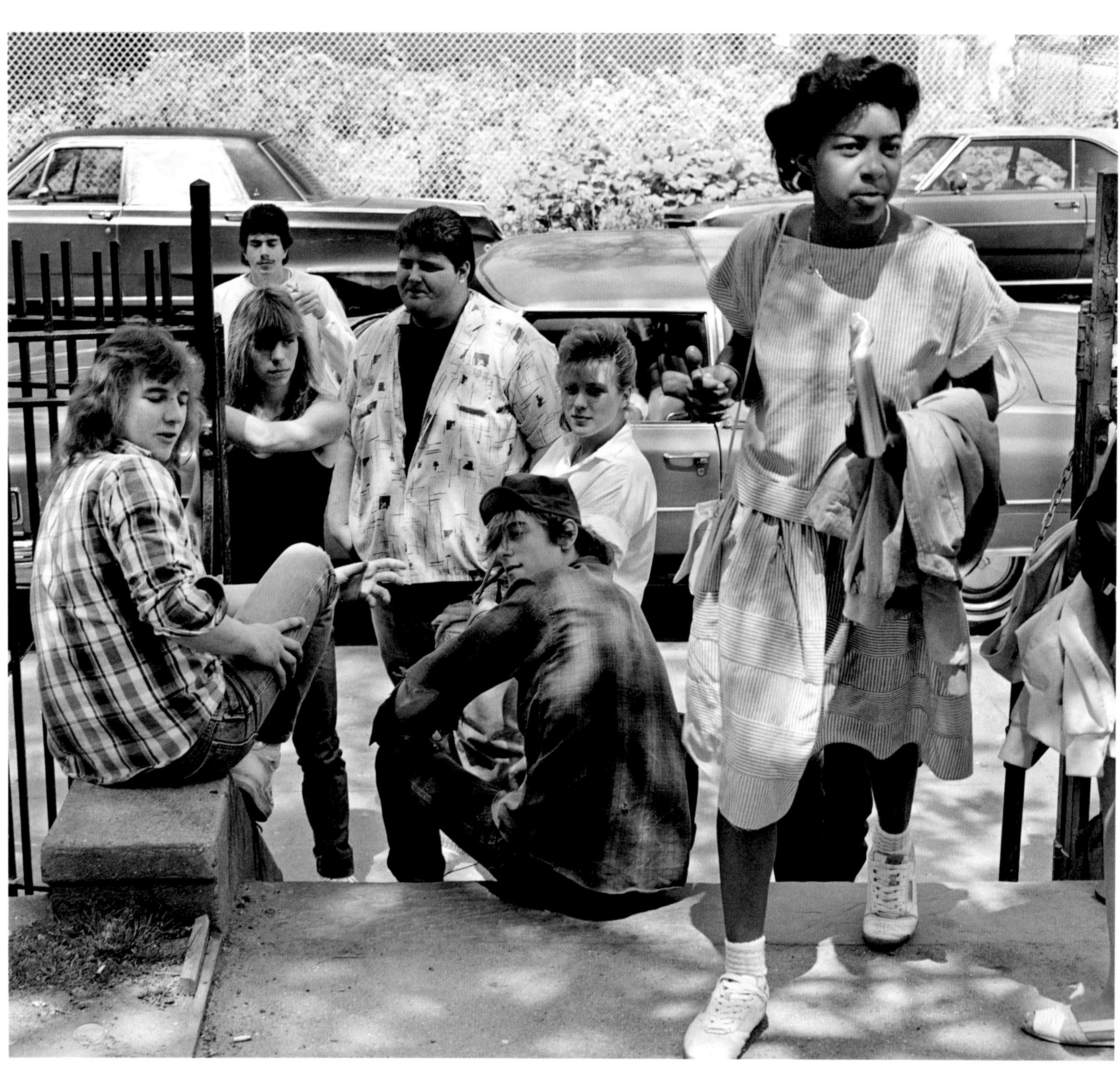

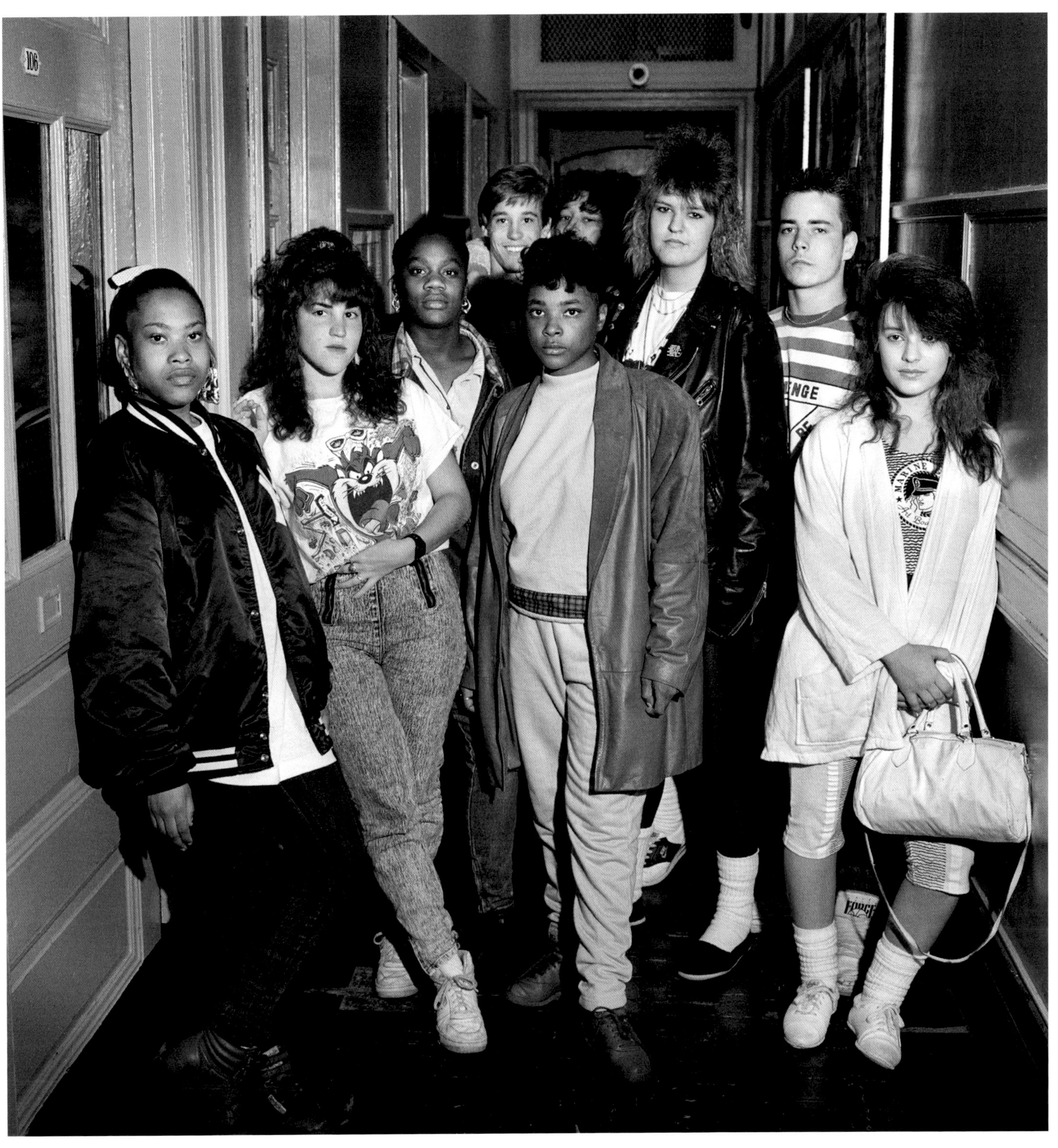

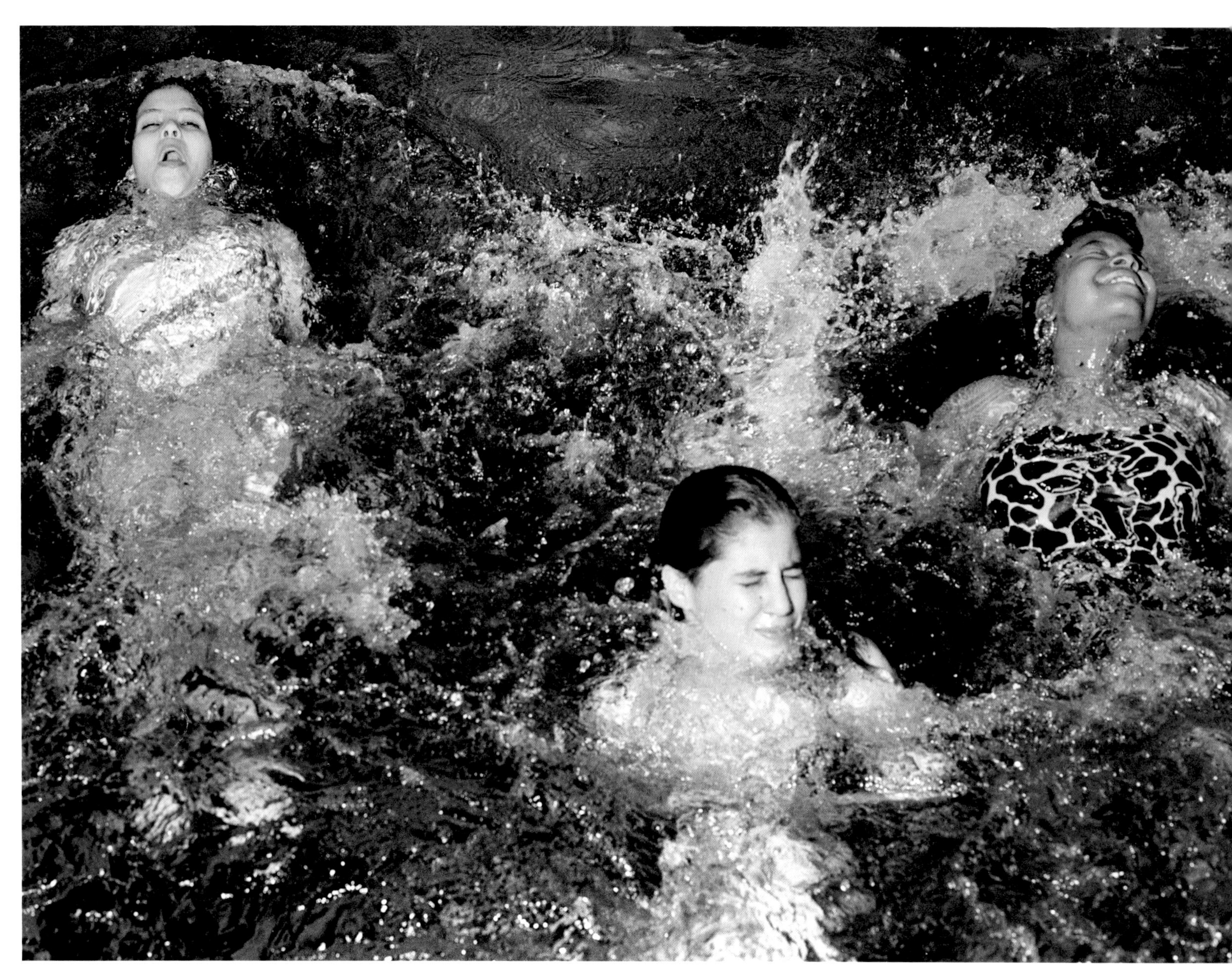

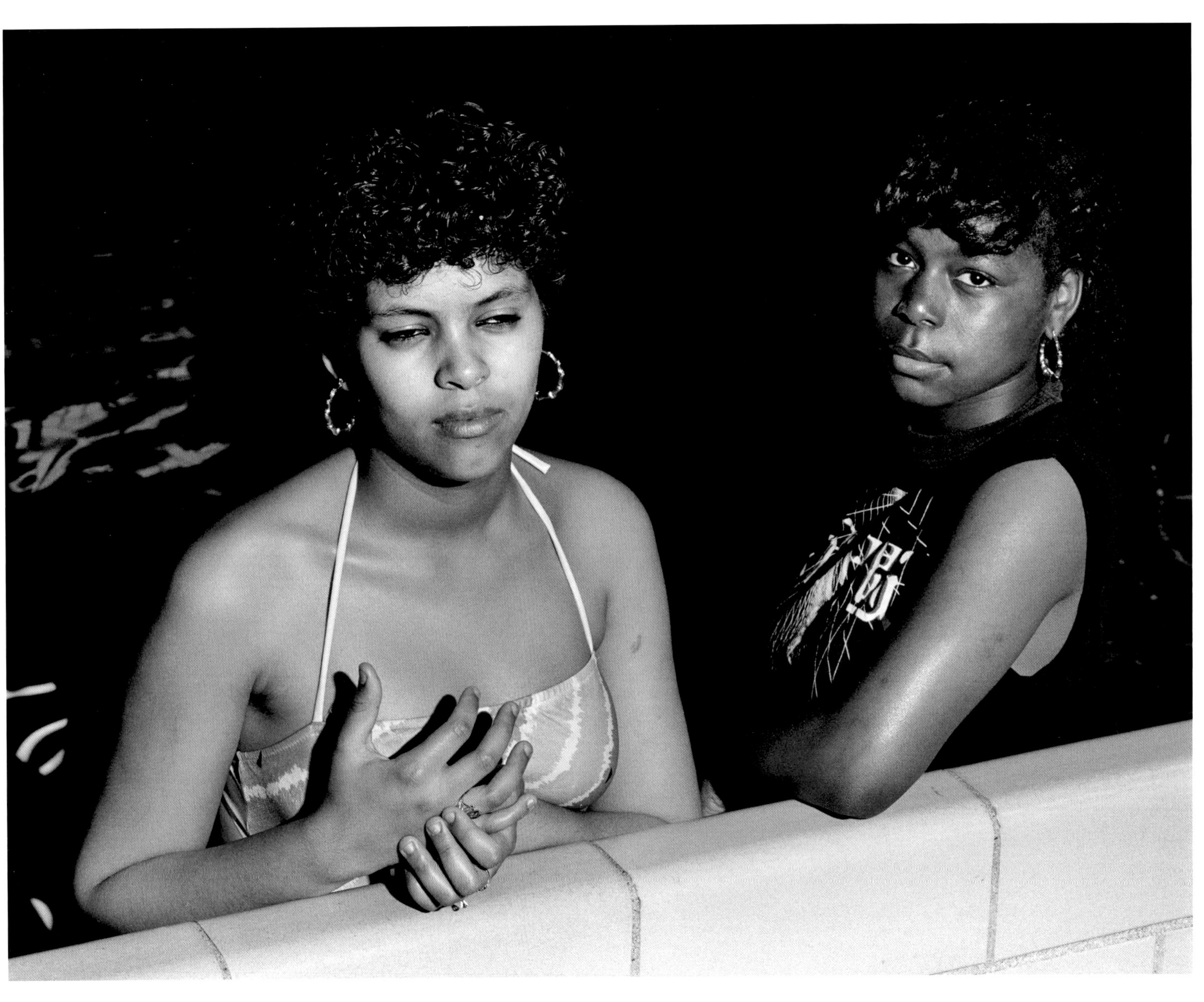

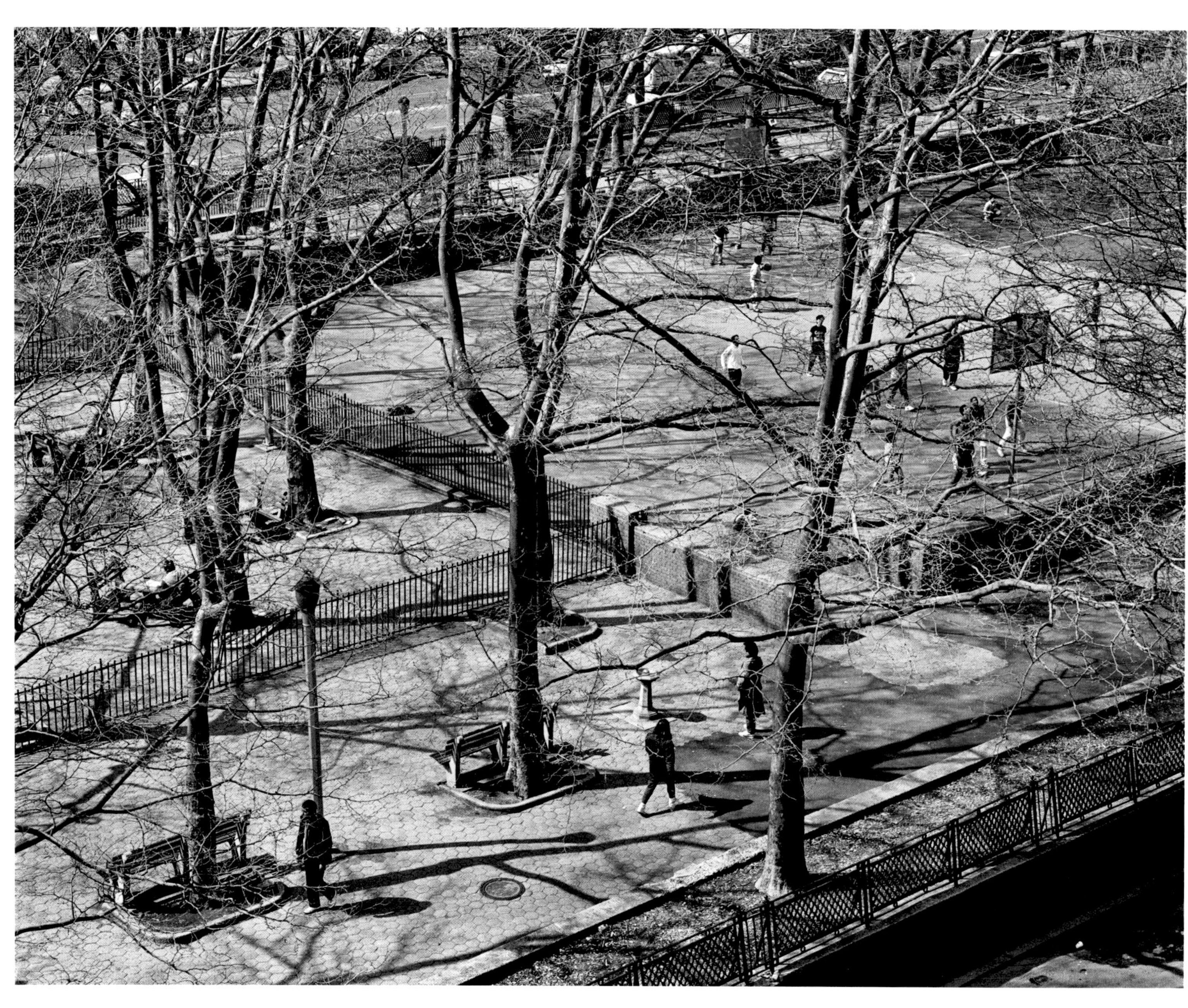

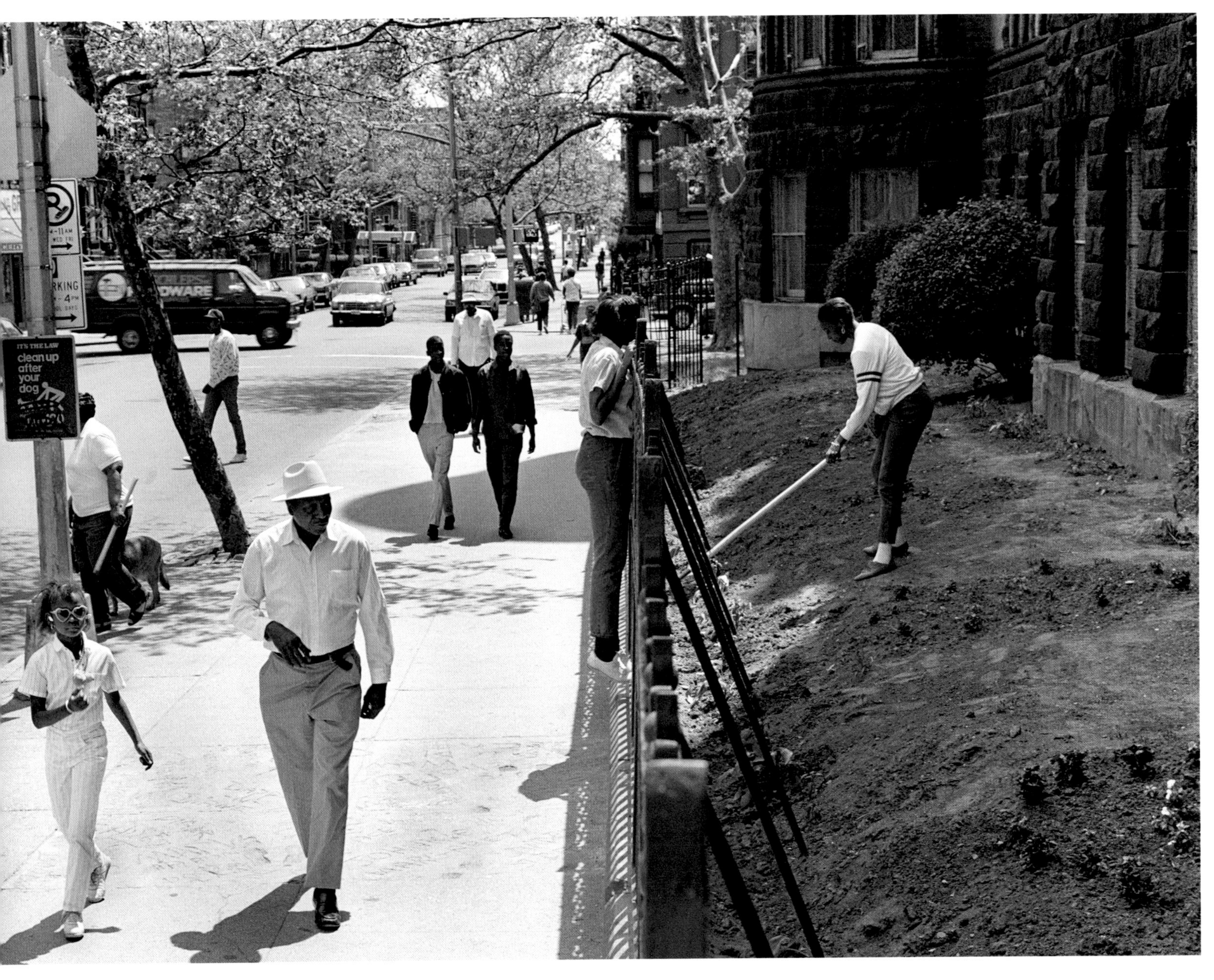

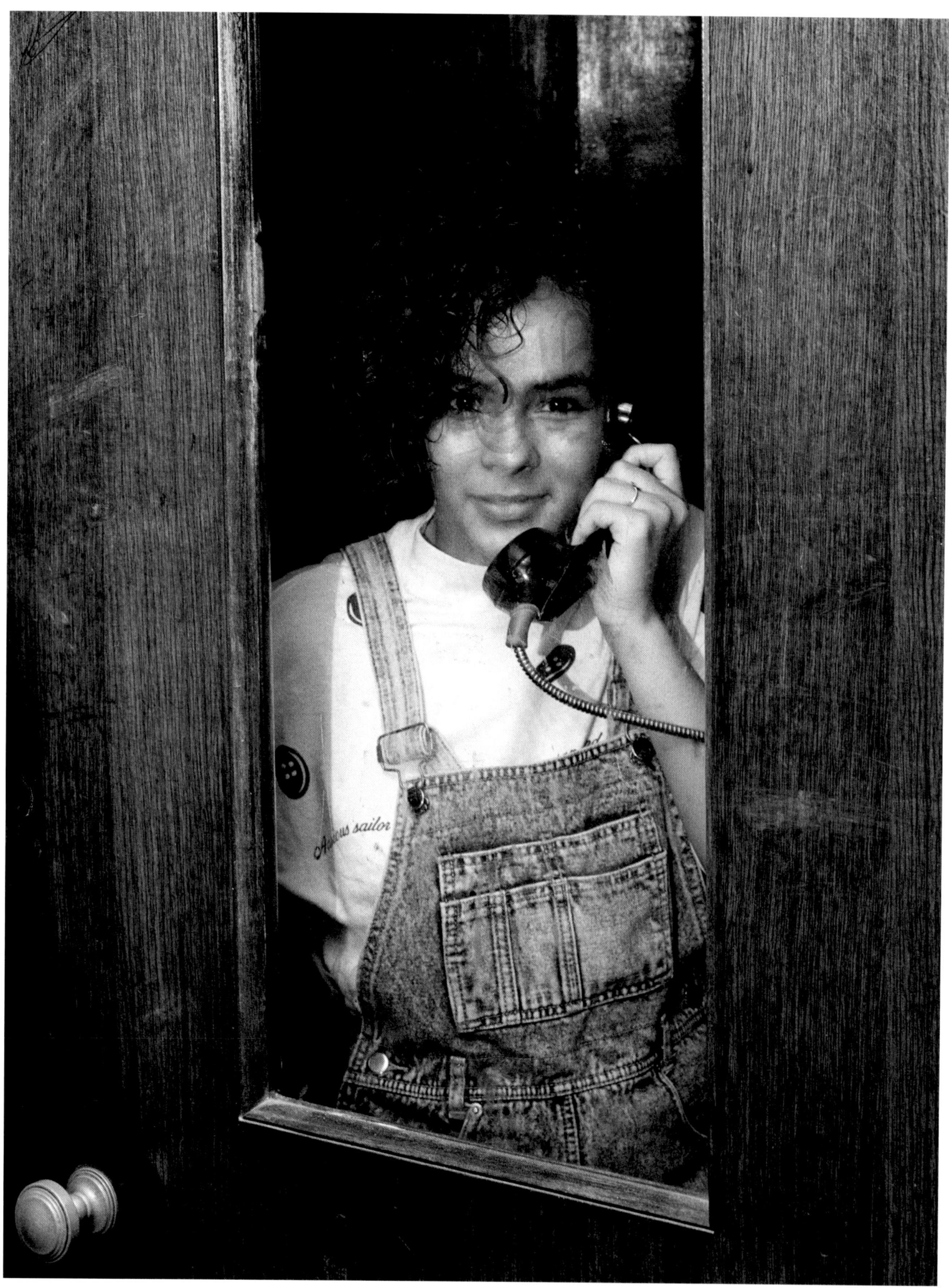

LIST OF PHOTOGRAPHS

11 - *Lower East Side Boys*, Manhattan, 1962

12 - *No World War Over Cuba,* march to Dag Hammarskjold Plaza, United Nations, Cuban Missile Crisis, Manhattan, October 1962

13 - *No War Over Cuba,* rally at Dag Hammarskjold Plaza, United Nations, Cuban Missile Crisis, Manhattan, October 1962

14 - *Dancing Girls*, East 68th Street, Manhattan, 1962

15 - *Freedom Sing,* sponsored by Brooklyn College NAACP in support of the southern civil rights movement, Brooklyn, ca. 1962

16 - *Protesting the Killing of Four African American Girls* in the Ku Klux Klan's bombing of the 16th Street Baptist Church in Birmingham, Alabama, on Sunday morning September 15th, 1963. These demonstrators picketed at Dag Hammarskjold Plaza, United Nations, to help focus the world's attention on the inhumanity of the segregationist terror tactics in Alabama led by Governor George Wallace, and to demand that President Kennedy send Federal troops to Birmingham to protect the rights and lives of its Black citizens. Manhattan, September 1963

17 - *Stop Murder in Birmingham*, protesting the killing of four African American girls in the Ku Klux Klan's bombing of the 16th Street Baptist Church in Birmingham, Alabama, on Sunday morning September 15th, 1963. These demonstrators picketed at Dag Hammarskjold Plaza, United Nations, to help focus the world's attention on the inhumanity of the segregationist terror tactics in Alabama led by Governor George Wallace, and to demand that President Kennedy send Federal troops to Birmingham to protect the rights and lives of its Black citizens. Manhattan, September 1963

18 - *School Children*, Harlem, Manhattan, 1963

19 - *Non-violent Civil Disobedience,* at a train station in Flushing, protesting against discriminatory job hiring at the 1964 World's Fair, Queens, April 1964

CITYWIDE SCHOOL BOYCOTT

23 - *Students with Signs,* at the citywide school boycott rally, near headquarters of the New York City Board of Education, Downtown Brooklyn, 1964

24 - *Picket Line in Support of Citywide School Boycott,* headquarters of the New York City Board of Education, 110 Livingston Street, Downtown Brooklyn, 1964

25 - *Students Picketing Their School,* in support of the school boycott, Lafayette High School, Bath Beach, Brooklyn, 1964

26 - *Puerto Rican / Labor Union March*, in support of the school boycott, Brooklyn Bridge, 1964

27 - *Malcolm X Speaking*, labor union/civil rights rally in support of the New York City school boycott, Upper East Side, Manhattan, 1964

62 - *Vietnam Veterans Against the War,* National Spring Mobilization to End the War in Vietnam, Manhattan, April 15, 1967

63 - *Front Line, Peace March,* National Spring Mobilization to End the War in Vietnam, with Norma Becker, head of the Fifth Avenue Peace Committee, and others, including political, union, and civil rights leaders. They were marching to rally in Central Park and then on to the United Nations, Manhattan, April 15, 1967

64 - *Carry On Rev. King's Work,* Veterans contingent, National Spring Mobilization to End the War in Vietnam, Manhattan, April 15, 1967

65 - *End Racial Oppression!* Student Mobilization Committee/Columbia University contingent National Spring Mobilization to End the War in Vietnam, Manhattan, April 15, 1967

66 - *Harlem Peace March,* National Spring Mobilization to End the War in Vietnam, Manhattan, April 15, 1967

67 - *Harlem Peace March With Brownstones,* National Spring Mobilization to End the War in Vietnam, Manhattan, April 15, 1967

68 - *We Mourn All the Dead,* Women Strike for Peace contingent, National Spring Mobilization to End the War in Vietnam, Manhattan, April 15, 1967

69 - *Vietnam for the Vietnamese,* National Spring Mobilization to End the War in Vietnam. Participating organizations, groups and individuals came from the five boroughs as well as from the Philadelphia, Boston, New Jersey, and Long Island regions, Manhattan, April 15, 1967

DR. MARTIN LUTHER KING, JR.

73 - *Dr. Martin Luther King, Jr. with Mrs. Du Bois Peck Williams,* Dr. W.E.B. Du Bois' only granddaughter, at the *Freedomways* reception after the Dr. W.E.B. Du Bois Centennial Tribute at Carnegie Hall, where Dr. King gave the keynote speech, Manhattan, February 23, 1968

75 - *Dr. Martin Luther King, Jr.* at the *Freedomways* Reception, after the Dr. W.E.B. Du Bois Centennial Tribute at Carnegie Hall, where Dr. King gave the keynote speech, Manhattan, February 23, 1968

OCEAN HILL BROWNSVILLE

79 - *A Young Organizer Sharing Black Panther Party Literature,* Rockaway Avenue, Brownsville, Brooklyn, 1969

80 - *Deborah Bold's Little Brother and His Friends,* Herkimer Street, Ocean Hill Brownsville, Brooklyn, ca. 1970

81 - *Girls at Gate,* Herkimer Street, Ocean Hill Brownsville, Brooklyn, ca. 1970

82 - *Girls in Their Own World,* Ocean Hill Brownsville, Brooklyn, 1969

83 - *Students Reading The Last Poetry of Langston Hughes* in *Freedomways,* Spring Issue, J.H.S. 271, in the Ocean Hill Brownsville experimental community controlled school district, Brooklyn, 1968

84 - *Three Boys Playing,* Ocean Hill Brownsville, Brooklyn, 1969

85 - *Brownsville, a*round the corner from the local Black Panther Party Headquarters, Brooklyn, 1969

89 - *Daisy with Madonna Gloves,* Bushwick, Brooklyn, 1987

90 - *Backyards,* George Street, from the Melrose Street rooftop of Bushwick Youth Services Bureau/Offsite Educational Services, Bushwick, Brooklyn, 1987

91 - *Snow on Melrose Street,* Bushwick, Brooklyn, 1981

92 - *Pigeon Coop,* Bushwick, Brooklyn, 1978

93 - *Benjamin Diaz with Pigeon,* Bushwick, Brooklyn, ca. 1979

94 - *Alejandro Gonzalez, Jr., Corey (Dee Dee) Martin, Edmond (Brownie) Huertas, Hector Garcia, and Jose Ben Santana,* Melrose Street, Bushwick, Brooklyn, 1978

95 - *Jacqueline Santiago and Cathy Lindsey,* Hart Street, Bushwick, Brooklyn, ca. 1976

96 - *Girl in White Dress,* Wilson Avenue and Troutman Street, Bushwick, Brooklyn, 1978

97 - *Roberto Mahones,* student, outside the small textile factory where he worked after school, Melrose Street, Bushwick, Brooklyn, 1987

98 - *Silvia Quinones,* Myrtle Avenue, Bushwick, Brooklyn, ca. 1981

99 - *"Linda," Raul Quinones' Toy Chihuahua,* Myrtle Avenue, Bushwick, Brooklyn, ca. 1981

100 - *Basketball, Bicycle, Girls' Gym Class,* I.S. 111 schoolyard, Bushwick, Brooklyn, ca. 1985

101 - *Basketball Ballet,* I.S. 111 schoolyard, Bushwick, Brooklyn, ca. 1981

102 - *Gushing Hydrant,* Melrose Street, Bushwick, Brooklyn, ca. 1985

103 - *Dunking,* I.S. 111 schoolyard, Bushwick, Brooklyn, ca. 1987

104 - *Jump Rope,* P.S. 145, Noll Street, Bushwick, Brooklyn, ca. 1984

105 - *Bicycle and Group,* Jefferson Street, Bushwick, Brooklyn, ca. 1987

106 - *Victor Garcia at Tameka's Candy Store,* Wilson Avenue, Bushwick, Brooklyn, 1978

107 - *Central Avenue Reflection,* Bushwick, Brooklyn, 1987

108 - *Pigeon Cloud,* Central Avenue, Bushwick, Brooklyn, 1987

109 - *Card Game,* Fermi Playground, adjacent to I.S. 111 schoolyard, Central Avenue and Troutman Street, Bushwick, Brooklyn, 1977

ALTERNATIVE HIGH SCHOOL STUDENTS

113 - *Tompkins Square Park Handball Courts,* students from the Puerto Rican Council, Offsite Educational Services Alternative High School Program (based at the nearby Jacob Riis Housing Project on Avenue D), East Village, Manhattan, 1988

114 - *Lunchtime Recess,* Concord High School, Rhine Avenue, Staten Island, 1987

115 - *Hallway Group,* Concord High School, Staten Island, 1989

116 - *Three University Heights High School Students,* Bronx Community College pool, Bronx, 1989

117 - *Two University Heights High School Students,* Bronx Community College pool, Bronx, 1989

118 - *Sarah Delano Roosevelt Park,* view from fourth floor office window of Satellite Academy High School, Forsyth Street, Lower East Side, Manhattan, 1989

119 - *Street Scene and Student Working on the School Garden*, outside the historic old Boys High School building which had become home to several New York City alternative high schools and high school programs, Madison Street, Bedford-Stuyvesant, Brooklyn, 1987

120 - *Girl in Telephone Booth,* summer school program for Satellite Academy, Bronx Regional High School and University Heights High School, Chambers Street, Manhattan, 1989

128- *North of Union Square*, Manhattan, ca. 1986

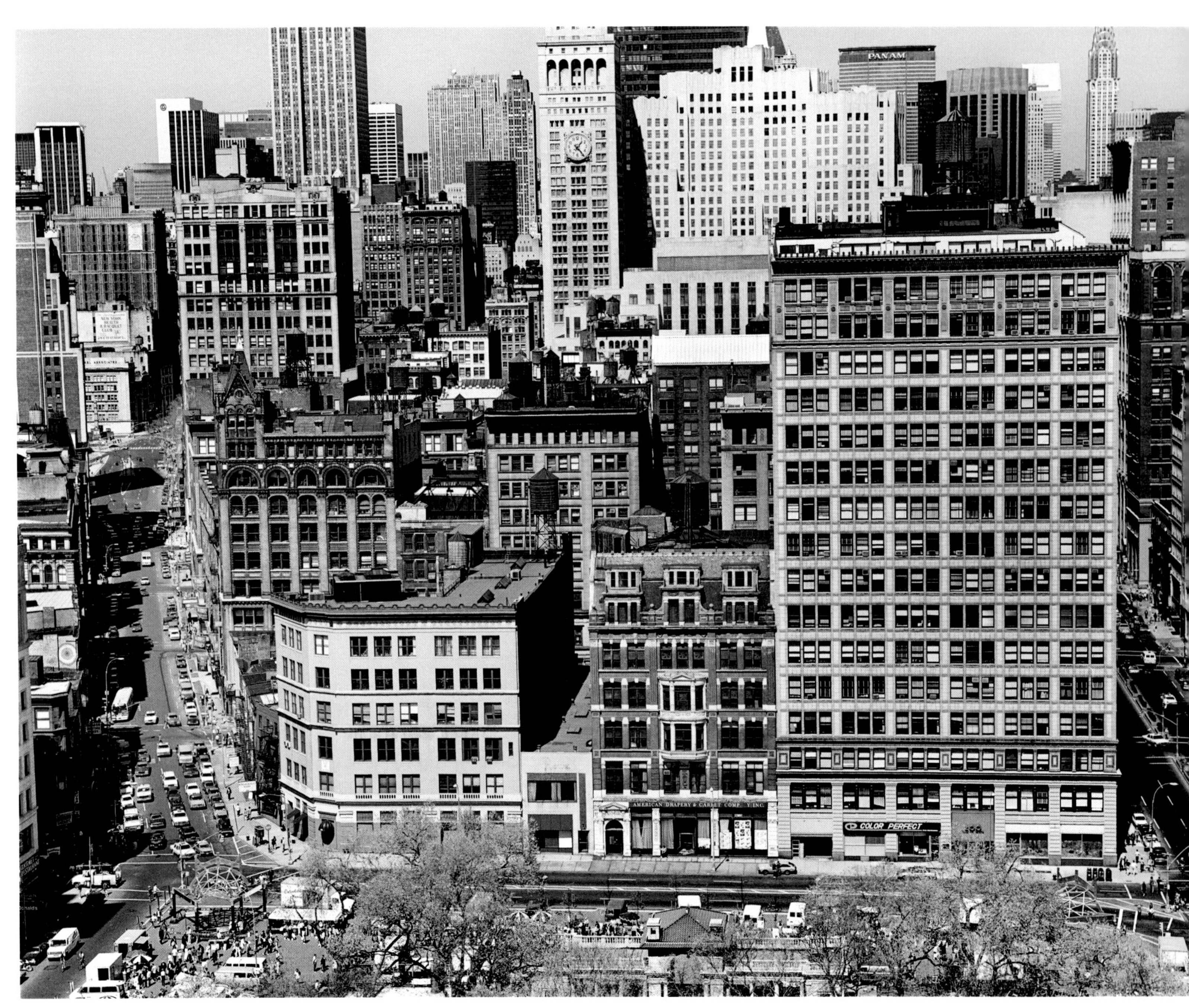

BIOGRAPHICAL SUMMARIES

BUILDER LEVY

Builder Levy was born in Florida in 1942 and raised in Brooklyn. He received a BA in art from Brooklyn College in 1964, where he studied painting with Ad Reinhardt, photography with Walter Rosenblum who became a mentor and friend, and art history with Milton Brown. He researched the Photo League, the photography program of the Farm Security Administration (FSA), and the Kamoinge Workshop in conjunction with his master's degree in art education at New York University in 1966. In the 1970s, close friendships with Paul Strand and Helen Levitt added insights into his role and possibilities as an artist. His experience as a New York City teacher of teenagers for 35 years also enriched his vision.

He was awarded Fellowships by the John Simon Guggenheim Memorial Foundation, Alicia Patterson Foundation, National Endowment for the Arts in Photography, Puffin Foundation, and a Furthermore publication grant by the J.M. Kaplan Fund. He received two commissions from the Appalachian College Association.

His three previous books are: *Images of Appalachian Coalfields*, foreword by Cornell Capa, Temple University Press, *Builder Levy Photographer*, essay by Naomi Rosenblum, A.R.T. Press, and *Appalachia USA*, David R. Godine publisher, foreword by Denise Giardina. His work is included in more than 40 other books and several films, including Ken Burns' and Lynn Novick's *The Vietnam War* PBS Series, and Raul Peck's *I Am Not Your Negro*, about James Baldwin and his relationship to Martin Luther King, Malcolm X, and Medgar Evers.

His photographs are in more than 80 collections including the Sir Elton John Photography Collection; Museum of Fine Arts, Houston; High Museum of Art; International Center of Photography; Metropolitan Museum of Art, Watson Library; Brooklyn Museum; Museum of the City of New York; Chrysler Museum of Art; John and Mable Ringling Museum of Art; Smithsonian African American Museum of History and Culture; Victoria and Albert Museum; Ruhrland Museum; and the Bibliothèque nationale de France.

His work has appeared in more than 250 exhibitions, including more than 60 one-person shows. He was included in *Road to Freedom: Photographs of the Civil Rights Movement, 1956–1968* at The High Museum of Art; *Women and the Civil Rights Movement*, Chrysler Museum of Art; *The Art of The Platinum Print*, the Peter Fetterman Gallery; *Everyday Beauty*, Smithsonian National Museum of African American History and Culture; *[Martin Luther] King in New York*, Museum of the City of New York; *One Place Understood, Photographs from the Do Good Fund*, Ogden Museum of Southern Art, New Orleans; his one person exhibition, *Appalachia USA* opened at the Ringling Museum of Art in Sarasota, in July 2015, and has been travelling since.

Levy's photographs and/or articles about him have appeared in more than 200 periodicals, including on four front covers and two back covers of the quarterly *Freedomways*.

Deborah Willis, Ph.D, is University Professor and Chair of the Department of Photography & Imaging at the Tisch School of the Arts at New York University and has an affiliated appointment with the College of Arts and Sciences, Department of Social & Cultural Analysis, Africana Studies, where she teaches courses on photography and imaging, iconicity, and cultural histories visualizing the black body, women, and gender. Her research examines photography's multifaceted histories, visual culture, the photographic history of Slavery and Emancipation, contemporary women photographers and beauty. She received the John D. and Catherine T. MacArthur Fellowship and was a Richard D. Cohen Fellow in African and African American Art, Hutchins Center, Harvard University; a John Simon Guggenheim Fellow, and an Alphonse Fletcher, Jr. Fellow. She has pursued a dual professional career as an art photographer and as one of the nation's leading historians of African American photography and curator of African American culture. Professor Willis received the NAACP Image Award in 2014 for her co-authored book (with Barbara Krauthamer) *Envisioning Emancipation*. Other notable projects include *Posing Beauty: African American Images from the 1890s to the Present, Out [o] Fashion Photography: Embracing Beauty, The Black Female Body A Photographic History, Reflections in Black: A History of Black Photographers – 1840 to the Present, Michelle Obama: The First Lady in Photographs*, and *Black Venus 2010: They Called Her 'Hottentot'*.

Tritone spot-varnished printing on Arctic Volume Ivory paper
by Grafiche Damiani Grafiche Damiani – Faenza Group SpA, Faenza, Italy.

Digital files by Andrew Jarman of Black and White on White,
Bushwick, Brooklyn.

Set in New Century Schoolbook and Franklin Gothic types.
Designed by Jerry Kelly, New York, NY.

————————————